BECKER
on
BRIDGE

BECKER on BRIDGE

by B. Jay Becker

GROSSET & DUNLAP, INC.
A NATIONAL GENERAL COMPANY

Publishers   New York

INTRODUCTION

When I started to select hands for this book from the daily columns I have written for King Features Syndicate over the past 15 years, it turned out that there were no less than 5400 articles for me to choose from. They had appeared in more than 500 newspapers scattered throughout the world.

My first object was to single out those articles that would best help the reader to understand the underlying thought processes that go into the making of a bridge player. However, a great many other hands have been included in this book simply because I thought they were either exceptionally interesting, or humorous, or because they were needed to create an altogether well-rounded book.

With few exceptions, the bidding is Standard American, that is, bids can generally be assumed to have their natural meaning. But the main thrust of the book is toward the play of the cards—as seen from both the declarer's and defenders' viewpoint. It is in this area—the play of the cards—that bridge reveals how thoroughly logical and fascinating a game it is. Wherever possible I have gone into the why and wherefore of the play instead of merely giving a recitation of how the play went. Card reading, endplays and coups of various sorts, percentage plays and many other techniques are heavily stressed, but more than anything else I have tried to demonstrate the rational and orderly thinking that dominates the approach to the play of a hand.

B. JAY BECKER

The Case of the Lowly Five

East dealer.
Both sides vulnerable.

NORTH
- ♠ Q J 7
- ♥ K Q
- ♦ A K Q
- ♣ K Q J 5 2

WEST
- ♠ 9 6
- ♥ 2
- ♦ 10 8 6 5 3 2
- ♣ 8 7 4 3

EAST
- ♠ K 8 5
- ♥ A J 9 8 7 6 3
- ♦ 4
- ♣ A 9

SOUTH
- ♠ A 10 4 3 2
- ♥ 10 5 4
- ♦ J 9 7
- ♣ 10 6

The bidding:

East	South	West	North
1 ♥	Pass	Pass	Dble
2 ♥	2 ♠	Pass	4 ♠

Opening lead—two of hearts.

When play commences, the ace is the highest card of each suit. As play progresses, other cards assume dominant rank as the higher ones are used up.

This process of promotion takes place in many deals and is easy enough to keep track of when the promoted cards are honors, but becomes somewhat difficult to follow when apparently insignificant cards suddenly assume the highest stature.

Here is a case where a lowly five proved to be the decisive card in the hand. South got to four spades after East had opened with one heart, and West led his singleton heart.

East took the queen with the ace and returned a low heart which West trumped with the six. West led back a club and East won with the ace and played the jack of hearts.

South had to follow with the ten and West made the fine defensive play of ruffing with the nine to force dummy's jack.

Declarer had lost three tricks by now and had to avoid the loss of a trump in order to make the contract. He led the queen of spades from dummy, and when East covered with the king, he won it with the ace, West showing out.

South then entered dummy by playing a diamond and led the seven of spades. But East, who had carefully observed his partner's early plays of the six and nine, covered the seven with the eight, forcing South's ten, and thus promoted his five so that it became the highest trump. Declarer had only the 4-3-2 left and had to go down one.

It would not have helped declarer to lead the seven from dummy originally, instead of the queen, because East would cover the seven with the eight and would still eventually make a trump trick with the five.

You wouldn't think, from looking at East's hand, that the five of spades would become the commanding card after only two rounds of trumps were played, but that's exactly what happened.

The Search for the Missing Queen

North dealer.
North-South vulnerable.

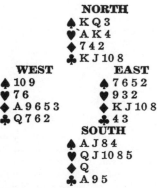

NORTH
♠ K Q 3
♥ A K 4
♦ 7 4 2
♣ K J 10 8

WEST
♠ 10 9
♥ 7 6
♦ A 9 6 5 3
♣ Q 7 6 2

EAST
♠ 7 6 5 2
♥ 9 3 2
♦ K J 10 8
♣ 4 3

SOUTH
♠ A J 8 4
♥ Q J 10 8 5
♦ Q
♣ A 9 5

The bidding:

North	East	South	West
1 NT	Pass	3 ♥	Pass
4 ♥	Pass	6 ♥	

Opening lead—ten of spades.

Every declarer periodically runs into the problem of the two-way finesse for a queen. Maybe there are players who welcome such problems and enjoy working them out, but I, for one, could do without the exercise very well.

However, you must be realistic about this business, since you do run into situations where you have to guess the direction in which to finesse, so let's look into the subject and see whether there are factors that might help your batting average on two-way finesses.

West leads the ten of spades and there you are with the slam in the bag if only you can guess which opponent has the queen of clubs. If you guess right, you can make six, maybe seven, but if you guess wrong, you go down one, losing a club and a diamond.

You take the spade with the queen and draw three rounds of trumps. Then you cash three more spade tricks. In the process, you discover that West started with two spades and two hearts, and East with four spades and three hearts. West discarded three diamonds as the spades and hearts were cashed.

Now comes the crucial play. About all there is to go on is the knowledge obtained from the opponents' plays to date. However, this knowledge, meager though it is, should lead you to the conclusion that West is the one more likely to have the queen of clubs.

West is known to have started with exactly nine cards in diamonds and clubs, whereas East cannot have had more than six cards in those suits.

West is consequently more likely to have club length than East, and therefore also has the greater chance to have been dealt the queen of clubs. Accordingly, you decide to finesse West for the queen, even though it is by no means a sure proposition.

You lead the ace of clubs, unblocking the ten from dummy, play the nine of clubs and finesse, then repeat the finesse, and wind up making seven.

Penny Wise, Pound Foolish

North dealer.
Both sides vulnerable.

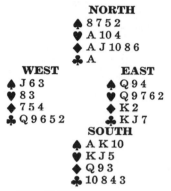

```
                    NORTH
                 ♠ 8 7 5 2
                 ♥ A 10 4
                 ♦ A J 10 8 6
                 ♣ A
   WEST                      EAST
♠ J 6 3                   ♠ Q 9 4
♥ 8 3                     ♥ Q 9 7 6 2
♦ 7 5 4                   ♦ K 2
♣ Q 9 6 5 2              ♣ K J 7
                    SOUTH
                 ♠ A K 10
                 ♥ K J 5
                 ♦ Q 9 3
                 ♣ 10 8 4 3
```

The bidding:

North	East	South	West
1 ♦	Pass	2 NT	Pass
3 NT			

Opening lead—five of clubs.

Probably the most valuable tool available to the defense during the play of the cards is the signal. If it were not that the defenders can signal encouragement or discouragement to each other by the play of high and low cards on a trick, perfect defense would be next to impossible.

Sometimes you hear people say that the play of a six or higher card is a signal of strength, while the play of a five or lower card is a signal of weakness. Although the idea behind this is valid, the statement is not really accurate.

It should be amended to say that the play of the lowest card you have is discouraging, while the play of a card which is not the lowest is encouraging. Thus, if partner leads the king of a suit in which you have a A-3-2, the play of the three is a signal for him to continue the suit even though the three, by itself, is not impressive as a high card.

Similarly, if partner leads the king and you have the 9-8-7 of the suit, the play of the seven is not a come-on signal. You cannot be held responsible for being dealt cards that prevent you from signaling in clear-cut fashion.

East failed to signal properly in the accompanying hand and the result was that South made three notrump instead of being defeated a trick.

West led a club. On dummy's ace East played the seven, but he should have played the jack. Declarer entered his hand with a spade, led the queen of diamonds and finessed.

East took the king, cashed the king of clubs, and returned the jack. West could not afford to overtake the jack, which would make South's ten a trick, and let the jack hold. Declarer then easily scored his game.

But if East had signaled with the jack, and thus unblocked the suit, the defenders would have been able to cash four club tricks and defeat the contract.

Once Upon a Time

South dealer.
Both sides vulnerable.

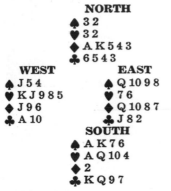

```
                NORTH
              ♠ 3 2
              ♥ 3 2
              ♦ A K 5 4 3
              ♣ 6 5 4 3
   WEST                   EAST
♠ J 5 4               ♠ Q 10 9 8
♥ K J 9 8 5           ♥ 7 6
♦ J 9 6               ♦ Q 10 8 7
♣ A 10                ♣ J 8 2
                SOUTH
              ♠ A K 7 6
              ♥ A Q 10 4
              ♦ 2
              ♣ K Q 9 7
```

The bidding:

South	West	North	East
1 ♠	2 ♥	3 ♦	Pass
4 ♥ (!)	Dble		

Opening lead — six of diamonds.

If you don't believe in fairy tales, then you won't believe this ever happened, but I have it on good authority that the deal was actually played in the early days of contract—specifically in 1927.

South opened the bidding with a spade. Of course, today, we'd bid a club to start, but in those days the idea of opening with the suit beneath the singleton had not yet been developed.

West overcalled with two hearts, a hair-raising experiment by present standards, but people were more sporting in those days. North entered the spirit of things with three diamonds, but at least he had an opening bid by South to rest on.

Now South was a very imaginative player who realized he would be unable to develop many diamond tricks if he undertook a three notrump contract, so he splashed into four hearts, even though West had already bid the suit. He thought he'd make enough high-card tricks in the side suits and low-card tricks in trumps to bring home four hearts.

West doubled of course—he couldn't stand being insulted—and led a diamond. South had no trouble making the contract —it was like taking candy from a baby. He won the diamond with the ace and cashed the king, discarding a club.

He then played a club, losing the king to the ace. Back came a club and South took the queen, cashed the A-K of spades, and ruffed a spade in dummy and a diamond in his hand.

By this time, South had won seven of the eight tricks played and was reduced to the A-Q-10 of hearts, a spade and a club. West had only trumps left.

Declarer led a spade and West was forced to ruff and return a trump. South won with the ten and this time played a club. Again West had to ruff and return a trump. So South made four hearts doubled.

Them was the days!

Look
Before
You Leap

South dealer.
Both sides vulnerable.

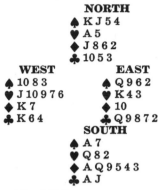

NORTH
♠ K J 5 4
♥ A 5
♦ J 8 6 2
♣ 10 5 3

WEST
♠ 10 8 3
♥ J 10 9 7 6
♦ K 7
♣ K 6 4

EAST
♠ Q 9 6 2
♥ K 4 3
♦ 10
♣ Q 9 8 7 2

SOUTH
♠ A 7
♥ Q 8 2
♦ A Q 9 5 4 3
♣ A J

The bidding:

South	West	North	East
1 ♦	Pass	1 ♠	Pass
2 NT	Pass	3 NT	

Opening lead—jack of hearts.

There are some hands you play in which you are sure from the word go that the contract will be made.

There are others in which the result is not predictable in advance because the outcome depends entirely on how the defenders' cards are divided.

The trick is to nail down those hands where the issue may seem to be in doubt, but which can be absolutely guaranteed with proper play. Here is a hand from that family.

South was in three notrump and West led a heart. Declarer ducked in dummy and East won the king. East saw no future in a heart continuation, since South was marked by the lead to have the queen of hearts, so he shifted to a club.

This turned out to be the killing blow. The jack lost to the king and a club return forced South's ace. When West later got in with a diamond, he led another club, and the upshot of the matter was that South went down two—200 points.

The fact is that South had one of those hands in which he could not be beaten—unless he beat himself. He made the mistake of ducking the heart lead and thereby dug his own grave.

There was a sure way of making the contract and no distribution of the adverse cards could defeat him. He should have played the ace of hearts on the first trick.

Declarer then leads the jack of diamonds and finesses if East plays low. (The jack is led to cover the possibility of East's having the K-10-7, in which case South loses no diamond tricks.)

If the finesse loses, West is on lead and can do South no harm. In the meantime, though, South has nine tricks available.

It is true that in most hands declarer would play low from dummy with this combination in hearts. But in this case, where the duck jeopardizes the contract and the ace play insures it, South has no real choice as to which play to make.

The Most Famous Liar in History

West dealer.
North-South vulnerable.

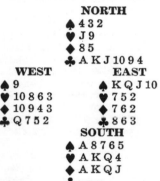

NORTH
♠ 4 3 2
♥ J 9
♦ 8 5
♣ A K J 10 9 4

WEST
♠ 9
♥ 10 8 6 3
♦ 10 9 4 3
♣ Q 7 5 2

EAST
♠ K Q J 10
♥ 7 5 2
♦ 7 6 2
♣ 8 6 3

SOUTH
♠ A 8 7 6 5
♥ A K Q 4
♦ A K Q J
♣ ——

The bidding:

West	North	East	South
Pass	1 NT	Pass	6 ♦

Opening lead—nine of spades.

Dear Mr. Becker: My name is Siegfried Munchausen. You may recall my illustrious father, who wrote the famous *Tall Tales of Baron Munchausen.* It is not generally known that my father, in addition to his many other high accomplishments, was undoubtedly the greatest bridge player in the world.

I give you here a sample of his exploits, which I encountered among his unpublished memoirs. He was playing at the time in the world championship, and his partner—naturally not of my father's class—contrived to land him in six diamonds.

This was not a good contract, but, as anyone can see, my father (South) had bid the hand perfectly. Remember, he was handicapped by having to contend with a partner who did not appreciate the fine art of scientific bidding.

West led a singleton spade. It is a peculiar thing, I might add, but many players in those days would foolishly attempt to defeat my father in any contract he happened to be playing. The West in this case found, to his sorrow—as had so many others before him—that this was next to impossible.

Baron Munchausen took the spade with the ace and drew four rounds of trumps, discarding two spades from dummy. He then played a low heart and, when West also played low, finessed the nine.

The nine won the trick, as my father was sure it would, and he next cashed the A-K of clubs, discarding the A-K of hearts from his hand. I realize that most players would have discarded their spades on the clubs, but this ridiculous type of play is what distinguished my father from less gifted players. If he had done this, he would have gone down.

Then my father led the jack of clubs from dummy and on it discarded the queen of hearts. West won the trick with the queen, but was forced to return a heart or a club to dummy, either of which plays gave my father the rest of the tricks and thus won him the world championship. Cordially and sincerely yours, S. Munchausen.

Simple Arithmetic

South dealer.
Neither side vulnerable.

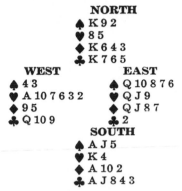

NORTH
♠ K 9 2
♥ 8 5
♦ K 6 4 3
♣ K 7 6 5

WEST
♠ 4 3
♥ A 10 7 6 3 2
♦ 9 5
♣ Q 10 9

EAST
♠ Q 10 8 7 6
♥ Q J 9
♦ Q J 8 7
♣ 2

SOUTH
♠ A J 5
♥ K 4
♦ A 10 2
♣ A J 8 4 3

The bidding:

South	West	North	East
1 NT	Pass	2 NT	Pass
3 NT			

Opening lead—six of hearts.

The Rule of Eleven can be used to advantage by either side. It has as its base the custom of leading the fourth best card of a suit.

In this hand, for example, when West leads the six of hearts—the fourth best of his long suit—it becomes possible for both East and South to apply the Rule of Eleven.

South subtracts six (the card led) from eleven. The answer five tells him there are five hearts higher than the six in the North, East and South hands.

Since South sees one of them in dummy and one in his hand, he knows that East has three hearts higher than the six. The knowledge does not help South in this particular deal, but that is the method he uses to obtain it.

East applies the Rule of Eleven in the same way. He also subtracts six from eleven and learns that North, East and South have five cards higher than the six. Since he has three higher and dummy one higher, East knows that declarer has only one heart better than the six.

East can make good use of this information in choosing his line of defense. After East plays the jack of hearts, which loses to the king, South leads a low club to the king and another club back. East has to discard on the second club and should play his queen of hearts!

When West takes his queen of clubs, he is then in position to cash his hearts and defeat the contract.

But suppose East is unfamiliar with the Rule of Eleven. Then he might discard the six of spades or seven of diamonds on the club lead, and in either case West would find it difficult to lead the ace of hearts to run his suit.

West would be afraid that declarer had started with the K-Q-x of hearts and might lead a spade or a diamond in response to East's discard of either of those suits. This would permit declarer to make the contract.

Changing
Losers
to Winners

North dealer.
Neither side vulnerable.

NORTH
♠ 6 5 4
♥ A 9 3
♦ A K 10 8 7
♣ 10 8

WEST
♠ J
♥ K J 8 7 5 2
♦ 4
♣ K Q J 6 3

EAST
♠ Q 10 9 2
♥ 10
♦ Q J 9 5 3
♣ 7 5 4

SOUTH
♠ A K 8 7 3
♥ Q 6 4
♦ 6 2
♣ A 9 2

The bidding:

North	East	South	West
1 ♦	Pass	1 ♠	2 ♥
Pass	Pass	3 ♣	Pass
4 ♠			

Opening lead—king of clubs.

Anyone can win tricks with aces and kings—the idea is to take them with deuces and treys.

Low-card tricks play a substantial role in many deals, but frequently their importance is not recognized. Look at this hand, for example, where low cards contribute heavily to the success of the contract.

West leads the king of clubs, which declarer ducks, and continues with the queen, which South takes with the ace.

Declarer's plan of play is now fairly automatic. He has a right to assume that the spades will break normally (3-2), and that the diamonds will be divided either 3-3 or 4-2.

He therefore plans to cash the A-K of spades and then proceed to establish the diamonds. If both suits are divided perfectly, he will wind up with eleven tricks.

But when he leads the A-K of spades, he discovers the 4-1 break and has to revise his thinking. The contract is now in danger and he must take steps to try to overcome the bad trump division.

Accordingly, he cashes the A-K of diamonds, discovering that there is also a 5-1 division of diamonds. However, this development, which earlier he would have regarded as unfavorable, is now actually beneficial. It points to a way to make the contract.

He ruffs a diamond, ruffs a club in dummy, and ruffs another diamond. Then, after entering dummy with a heart, he trumps the last diamond.

By now, he has made ten tricks and the contract. They consist of the six tricks scored with aces and kings, and the four he scored with low cards, all trumps.

It will be observed that South theoretically had five losers— two spades, two hearts and a club—and yet made ten tricks.

By manipulating his cards to the best advantage, and especially by timing his plays exactly and scoring four tricks with low cards, declarer is able to win ten tricks. In effect, South telescopes his five losers so that they become only three.

Executing a Squeeze

North dealer.
North-South vulnerable.

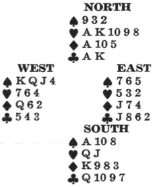

NORTH
♠ 9 3 2
♥ A K 10 9 8
♦ A 10 5
♣ A K

WEST
♠ K Q J 4
♥ 7 6 4
♦ Q 6 2
♣ 5 4 3

EAST
♠ 7 6 5
♥ 5 3 2
♦ J 7 4
♣ J 8 6 2

SOUTH
♠ A 10 8
♥ Q J
♦ K 9 8 3
♣ Q 10 9 7

The bidding:

North	East	South	West
1♥	Pass	2 NT	Pass
6 NT			

Opening lead—king of spades.

Among the advanced plays in bridge, the squeeze is one of the most difficult of all to execute.

Three important elements are generally necessary for the successful execution of a squeeze.

1. One defender (sometimes both) must have two suits to guard.

2. Declarer must have proper communication between his own hand and dummy.

3. Declarer must be in a position to win all the remaining tricks but one.

This last requirement is the one that alerts declarer to the possibility of a squeeze. Let's see how it applies to the present hand.

West leads the king of spades and South counts eleven sure winners. This means he can win eleven of the thirteen tricks that remain to be played, that is, all but two. In order to establish a squeeze situation, he ducks the king of spades, which then brings him to the all-but-one position.

Let's say West continues with the queen of spades (no other play affects the result). South takes it with the ace and cashes five heart tricks, discarding a spade and two diamonds from his hand. East is forced to discard a spade and a diamond in order to keep the clubs guarded. West, in the meantime, discards a spade and a club.

These are the remaining cards at this point:

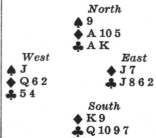

North
♠ 9
♦ A 10 5
♣ A K

West
♠ J
♦ Q 6 2
♣ 5 4

East
♦ J 7
♣ J 8 6 2

South
♦ K 9
♣ Q 10 9 7

Declarer cashes the A-K of clubs and plays a low diamond to the king. When he then leads the queen of clubs, West, with two suits to guard, cannot discard successfully. If he discards a spade, dummy discards a diamond; if he discards a diamond, dummy discards a spade. There is no escape from the squeeze.

Sylvia
Learns
Blackwood

South dealer.
Both sides vulnerable.

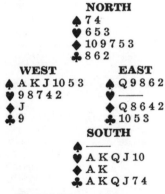

NORTH
♠ 7 4
♥ 6 5 3
♦ 10 9 7 5 3
♣ 8 6 2

WEST
♠ A K J 10 5 3
♥ 9 8 7 4 2
♦ J
♣ 9

EAST
♠ Q 9 8 6 2
♥ —
♦ Q 8 6 4 2
♣ 10 5 3

SOUTH
♠ —
♥ A K Q J 10
♦ A K
♣ A K Q J 7 4

The bidding:

South	West	North	East
2 ♥	2 ♠	Pass	3 ♥
4 NT	Pass	5 ♣	Pass
7 ♣			

Sylvia's astonishing adventures at the club would undoubtedly comprise an excellent anthology on how not to play the game, but such a compilation, if published, would inevitably be regarded as simply the product of a wild imagination instead of the actual incidents on which it would be based.

When she started to play at the club, Sylvia's conception of the game was something that had to be seen to be believed. It was not that Sylvia made her many astounding bids or plays in an effort to be brilliant, but only that her peculiar and tangential form of reasoning led her to what could politely be described as eccentric conclusions.

Sylvia tried her level best to conform to the frenzied advice her partners so volubly expounded, but they never knew what interpretations she would place upon their remonstrations when the next hand was dealt. This was especially true whenever Sylvia learned a new convention; no one could possibly predict the havoc that might result from her personalized use of it.

Nevertheless, Sylvia occasionally accomplished a *tour de force* as a result of her meanderings. For example, take this hand which arose right after she took up Blackwood.

Sylvia was South and opened two hearts. West bid two spades and East three hearts, at which point Sylvia branched out into Blackwood. Why she wanted to learn how many aces her partner had is impossible to explain, but, having learned a new convention, Sylvia was determined to make use of it.

North, with no aces, responded five clubs, which Sylvia raised to seven. East led a spade and North scored 2,240 points with his hand.

Sylvia's opponents were understandably upset by the outcome, and all the more so when they realized that had Sylvia first bid clubs instead of North, West would have been on lead and would have defeated the contract by leading a heart, which East's cuebid called for.

Road Map

East dealer.
Both sides vulnerable.

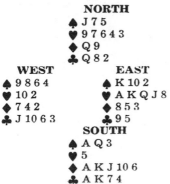

NORTH
- ♠ J 7 5
- ♥ 9 7 6 4 3
- ♦ Q 9
- ♣ Q 8 2

WEST
- ♠ 9 8 6 4
- ♥ 10 2
- ♦ 7 4 2
- ♣ J 10 6 3

EAST
- ♠ K 10 2
- ♥ A K Q J 8
- ♦ 8 5 3
- ♣ 9 5

SOUTH
- ♠ A Q 3
- ♥ 5
- ♦ A K J 10 6
- ♣ A K 7 4

The bidding:

East	South	West	North
1 ♥	Dble.	Pass	1 ♠
Pass	3 ♦	Pass	4 ♦
Pass	5 ♦		

Opening lead—ten of hearts.

You don't see the defenders' hands when you are the declarer, but as play progresses it often becomes possible to diagnose their respective holdings and thus play the hand to the best advantage.

Here is a case that shows how it's done. South is in five diamonds and West leads the ten of hearts. East overtakes with the jack and continues with the ace.

Declarer ruffs high and enters dummy with a diamond to lead a low spade to the queen. The finesse succeeds, as South has a right to expect from the bidding, and he then plays out all his trumps. That produces the following position:

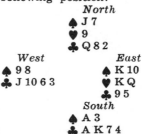

North
- ♠ J 7
- ♥ 9
- ♣ Q 8 2

West
- ♠ 9 8
- ♣ J 10 6 3

East
- ♠ K 10
- ♥ K Q
- ♣ 9 5

South
- ♠ A 3
- ♣ A K 7 4

Declarer hopes that the clubs are divided 3-3, but he also knows that if they are not he is still sure to make the hand. There is no possible combination of cards that can defeat him.

Accordingly, he cashes the A-K of clubs and plays a club to the queen. East shows out on the third club and is forced to discard a heart. He cannot spare a spade, because that would permit declarer to lead a low spade and catch the king.

South now knows that East has the K-x of spades and the king of hearts left. He knows that East started with five hearts, three diamonds, two clubs, and hence, three spades.

He therefore leads the nine of hearts from dummy and on it discards his club. East wins the heart with the king, but is then compelled to lead a spade, permitting South to win the last two tricks with the jack and ace. The defense wins two heart tricks in the hand, but no more.

17

Don't Fall Asleep at the Switch

North dealer.
North-South vulnerable.

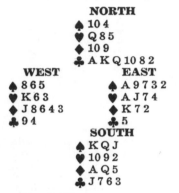

NORTH
♠ 10 4
♥ Q 8 5
♦ 10 9
♣ A K Q 10 8 2

WEST
♠ 8 6 5
♥ K 6 3
♦ J 8 6 4 3
♣ 9 4

EAST
♠ A 9 7 3 2
♥ A J 7 4
♦ K 7 2
♣ 5

SOUTH
♠ K Q J
♥ 10 9 2
♦ A Q 5
♣ J 7 6 3

The bidding:

North	East	South	West
1 ♣	Dble.	Redble.	1 ♦
Pass	Pass	2 NT	Pass
3 NT			

Opening lead—four of diamonds.

Good defensive play is the most difficult part of bridge for many players. Defense requires very close attention if it is to be really effective, and anyone who thinks it can be treated casually is bound to have his comeuppance once in a while.

Look at this hand where East has to do lots of thinking to find the right defense. West leads a diamond and East plays the king which South takes with the ace.

Right at this point East should draw certain conclusions about the hand. He knows from West's lead of the four (his fourth best diamond) that West's diamonds cannot be more than five cards in length.

He also knows that South has either the queen or jack of diamonds because, if South had only A-x-x of diamonds, he would not win the trick immediately but would hold off until the third round of the suit.

East likewise knows that if declarer has all the missing high cards, there is no hope of defeating the contract. He must therefore credit West with at least one high card. Furthermore, that card must be the king of hearts or else the hand is lost.

So when South leads a club to the queen at trick two and returns the ten of spades from dummy, East cannot afford to duck in the hope that declarer will take a finesse and lose the trick to West.

Instead, he should go right up with the ace and return a low heart on the theory that West has the king. If he does this and West wins and returns a heart, South is defeated.

But if East is asleep at the switch and ducks the ten of spades when it is led, he will rue the day because South then runs home with nine tricks.

This type of thinking, where a defender is forced to make certain assumptions and draw appropriate conclusions, is fairly common in defense. You just can't afford to be lazy in this field of endeavor.

The Key to Slam Bidding

South dealer.
North-South vulnerable.

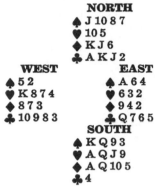

NORTH
- ♠ J 10 8 7
- ♥ 10 5
- ♦ K J 6
- ♣ A K J 2

WEST
- ♠ 5 2
- ♥ K 8 7 4
- ♦ 8 7 3
- ♣ 10 9 8 3

EAST
- ♠ A 6 4
- ♥ 6 3 2
- ♦ 9 4 2
- ♣ Q 7 6 5

SOUTH
- ♠ K Q 9 3
- ♥ A Q J 9
- ♦ A Q 10 5
- ♣ 4

The bidding:

South	West	North	East
1 ♠	Pass	3 ♠	Pass
4 NT	Pass	5 ♦	Pass
6 ♠			

Opening lead—ten of clubs.

An opening bid facing an opening bid means a game. An opening bid *plus* facing an opening bid *plus* means a slam. A *plus,* in this sense, means about a king more than a minimum opening bid.

North has an opening bid and a spade fit facing his partner's opening bid, so he jumps to three spades, which is forcing to game. (The jump raise shows a 13 to 15 point hand.)

South has 18 points in high cards, but after North announces a trump fit by jumping to three spades, South's hand can be re-appraised as having a value of about 21 points.

One way for South to judge the possibility of a slam is to add his point count to his partner's presumed point count, and, if the total comes to 33 or more and there is satisfactory control of each suit, assume there is a good chance for a slam.

An alternative way for South to assess his chances is to say he has two pluses more than an opening bid and that he is therefore in the slam zone.

The Blackwood is used to make sure that partner has at least one ace. When North shows one ace by responding five diamonds, South goes to a slam even though he knows the opponents have an ace. He has the intermediate strength that is sure to provide at least a reasonable chance to make twelve tricks.

West leads a club. At first blush, it would seem that South has to rely upon a heart finesse. Actually, this is not the case.

Declarer wins the club with the ace and ruffs a low club high. He then plays the three of spades to the seven. Assume East takes the ace and returns a heart.

South wins with the ace, leads the nine of spades to the ten, and ruffs the jack of clubs with his last trump. He enters dummy with a diamond and cashes the J-8 of spades and king of clubs, discarding the Q-J-9 of hearts. His diamonds then take the rest of the tricks.

Forewarned
Is
Forearmed

North dealer.
Neither side vulnerable.

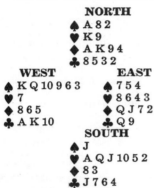

NORTH
♠ A 8 2
♥ K 9
♦ A K 9 4
♣ 8 5 3 2

WEST
♠ K Q 10 9 6 3
♥ 7
♦ 8 6 5
♣ A K 10

EAST
♠ 7 5 4
♥ 8 6 4 3
♦ Q J 7 2
♣ Q 9

SOUTH
♠ J
♥ A Q J 10 5 2
♦ 8 3
♣ J 7 6 4

The bidding:

North	East	South	West
1 ♦	Pass	1 ♥	1 ♠
Pass	Pass	2 ♥	2 ♠
3 ♥	Pass	4 ♥	

Opening lead—king of spades.

You shouldn't rush ahead without organizing a plan of play if you expect to get good results as declarer. Thoughtless, automatic plays may work well in some games, but not in bridge. There's no time clock at the bridge table that compels you to proceed without looking ahead to where you're going or what you may encounter.

Take this hand, which requires some foresight. South was in four hearts and West led a spade. Declarer took the king with the ace and drew four rounds of trumps. He had nine tricks in sight, and the only practical chance he then had to make the contract was to try to develop a club trick.

Accordingly, he led a club at this point. West took it with the ten and returned a spade. Declarer ruffed and led another club. West won the king and played a spade again. South ruffed with his last trump.

Declarer was now finished. He could have cashed the A-K of diamonds and settled for down one, but in an effort to make the contract, he led another club. West took the ace, and also the two spades he had left, and South went down two.

However, he should have made the contract. South had failed to make proper allowance for the possibility that the trumps might be divided 4-1 and that it would be necessary in such case to play four rounds of hearts to extract them. He should have started the clubs before tackling trumps.

If he had done this, the contract would have come home. Declarer should have led a club at trick two. The defense can do no better than take it and return a spade.

Declarer ruffs and leads another club. Again the defense takes the club and returns a spade. South ruffs and leads still another club. Now, when West wins the club, he is helpless. A spade return can be ruffed in dummy, while any other return permits South to win, draw trumps, and claim ten tricks.

The Art of Card Reading

East dealer.
North-South vulnerable.

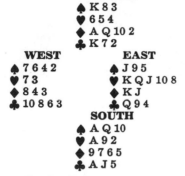

NORTH
♠ K 8 3
♥ 6 5 4
♦ A Q 10 2
♣ K 7 2

WEST
♠ 7 6 4 2
♥ 7 3
♦ 8 4 3
♣ 10 8 6 3

EAST
♠ J 9 5
♥ K Q J 10 8
♦ K J
♣ Q 9 4

SOUTH
♠ A Q 10
♥ A 9 2
♦ 9 7 6 5
♣ A J 5

The bidding:

East	South	West	North
1 ♥	Dble	Pass	3 ♦
Pass	3 NT		

Opening lead—seven of hearts.

Hands that are sure to make are no great challenge to the declarer. The fun comes from hands where the contract is in doubt and declarer has to work out his own salvation.

South is in three notrump and West leads a heart. The question is how South should play the hand. It is not actually difficult if you think about the matter, but it does require some care.

The first thing declarer does is count his sure tricks. He sees only seven—three spades, a heart, a diamond and two clubs—and therefore requires two more.

One way of gaining a trick is to take a club finesse, playing East for the queen, and another way of acquiring a trick is to take a diamond finesse, playing West for the king.

But before South goes ahead with either finesse, he must give thought to the likely location of these key cards. A little reflection should convince him that East has both the queen of clubs and king of diamonds. He reaches this conclusion because he sees 27 points in dummy's hand and his own, and it is not unreasonable to assume that East has the remaining 13 points, since he was the one who opened the bidding.

Declarer therefore proceeds with the play just as though he were looking at the opponents' cards. He lets East win the first heart with the ten and then takes the king with the ace.

He next plays a club to the king and finesses the jack on the return. He then cashes the ace of clubs and the A-K-Q of spades, observing that East follows suit to every play.

The trap is now sprung. Declarer leads a heart, permitting East to cash his remaining hearts, but East is then forced to lead a diamond from his K-J into dummy's A-Q. East makes four tricks in all, but South makes the contract. The plan that South formulates at the beginning pays off at the end.

Triple Action

South dealer.
Both sides vulnerable.

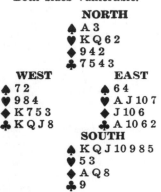

```
                NORTH
                ♠ A 3
                ♥ K Q 6 2
                ♦ 9 4 2
                ♣ 7 5 4 3
   WEST                    EAST
   ♠ 7 2                   ♠ 6 4
   ♥ 9 8 4                 ♥ A J 10 7
   ♦ K 7 5 3               ♦ J 10 6
   ♣ K Q J 8               ♣ A 10 6 2
                SOUTH
                ♠ K Q J 10 9 8 5
                ♥ 5 3
                ♦ A Q 8
                ♣ 9
```

The bidding:

South	West	North	East
4 ♠	Pass	Pass	Pass

Opening lead—king of clubs.

Let's say you're declarer at four spades and West leads the king of clubs and continues with a club which you ruff. There is some danger of going down because you may lose a heart and two diamonds if the adverse cards are divided unfavorably.

This being the case, you look for the line of play that offers the best chance of making the contract. One outstanding possibility is that West was dealt the ace of hearts, in which case there is a good chance of making a tenth trick by leading twice towards the K-Q of hearts.

It would not be wise to draw trumps first and then lead a heart. West might have the ace and duck the first heart lead and take the second one, and you would then have no entry to dummy to cash the remaining high heart.

To capitalize on the possibility that West was dealt the ace of hearts, you play a heart at trick three. However, East takes the queen with the ace and returns a club which you ruff.

This is an unfavorable development, of course, but you still have some strings left in your bow. With a little luck you may be able to hold yourself to one diamond loser.

There is no particular reason not to draw trumps now, so you cash the king and play a spade to the ace. Then you lead a low diamond from dummy planning to take a finesse.

When East follows low, you finesse, all right, but with the eight. Much to your satisfaction, the eight draws the king and your troubles are over. The triple finesse (a finesse against three missing high cards) succeeds.

It would not have helped East to play the ten on the diamond lead. You would play the queen, losing to the king, and later trap East's jack by finessing the eight.

Note that directly finessing the queen would defeat you. The advantage of the triple finesse is that it gives you two chances instead of one. It succeeds whenever East has the king or the J-10.

Taking
Out
Insurance

East dealer.
Both sides vulnerable.

NORTH
♠ J 10 4
♥ A 7 4
♦ 6 3
♣ K Q 10 5 2

WEST
♠ A Q 8 6 3
♥ 9 2
♦ J 10 7 2
♣ 9 4

EAST
♠ 7 5
♥ Q J 10 8
♦ Q 9 5
♣ J 7 6 3

SOUTH
♠ K 9 2
♥ K 6 5 3
♦ A K 8 4
♣ A 8

The bidding:

East	South	West	North
Pass	1 NT	Pass	3 NT

Opening lead—six of spades.

Many contracts stand or fall depending solely on how the defenders' cards are divided. The declarer has no control over the outcome of such hands and has to rely entirely on the luck of the deal.

But some contracts that appear to depend only on luck can be made by substituting the element of skill. Here is such a hand.

South is playing three no-trump and West leads a spade. The jack wins the trick and the question is how declarer should proceed.

South can count eight sure tricks at this point—a spade, two hearts, two diamonds and two hearts, two diamonds and three clubs. His best prospect for additional tricks lies in clubs, where he may be able to win one or two more tricks depending on how the missing clubs are divided.

Note what would happen in this hand if South played a club to the ace and then cashed the K-Q of clubs. He would discover that the clubs were divided 4-2, with East having four to the jack. He would then be unable to make the contract regardless of which way he turned.

Of course, this result could be charged to bad luck, since the contract would have been made if the clubs were divided 3-3, or if they were divided 4-2 with West having the club length. In the latter case, South would give up a club trick to West and thus safely develop his ninth trick.

But South has a better line of play available that substantially increases his chances of making the contract. What he should do is lead a low club from dummy at trick two, and when East plays low, finesse the eight.

True, the eight loses to the nine, but West, on lead, can do nothing to stop the contract. South is able to cash four club tricks as soon as he obtains the lead. The finesse of the eight into the safe hand assures the contract against any 4-2 (or 3-3) division.

The Power of Positive Thinking

North dealer.
Both sides vulnerable.

NORTH
♠ K Q J 10
♥ A K
♦ 9 3
♣ A K 7 5 2

WEST
♠ 3
♥ 10 5 4
♦ A 10 7 6 4 2
♣ 9 8 3

EAST
♠ A 8 7 6 5 2
♥ 7 3
♦ Q J 5
♣ 10 4

SOUTH
♠ 9 4
♥ Q J 9 8 6 2
♦ K 8
♣ Q J 6

The bidding:

North	East	South	West
1♣	Pass	1♥	Pass
2♠	Pass	3♥	Pass
4♥			

Opening lead — three of spades.

You can't play bridge and do well if you adopt the attitude that you're licked when you start. It's much better to play each hand on the basis that there's a chance of making the contract (if you're the declarer) or of defeating the contract (if you're a defender).

This approach is bound to win many points for you, or, at least, save you a bushelful. The principle we're discussing asserts itself in many, many hands, and all you have to do is look for the right time and the right way to apply it.

West led a spade and East had no trouble diagnosing the lead as a singleton. So he won with the ace and returned a spade for West to ruff. West then cashed the ace of diamonds—he would have lost it if he hadn't — and that was the end of the hand. South made exactly four hearts.

It will be noted that East could have defeated the contract by returning the queen of diamonds at trick two instead of a spade. Whether or not South covered the queen with the king, the defense would take the first four tricks.

The question is whether East should have known this and should have by-passed the opportunity to give West an immediate spade ruff in order to first lead a diamond.

The answer is clearly in favor of leading the queen of diamonds at trick two. East has to play on the basis that West has the ace of diamonds. East must assume that this is the case; otherwise, he might as well fold up his cards and concede the contract.

It is true that if South had held the ace of diamonds, East would have cost his side a 30-point trick by failing to return a spade, but this would be a trivial loss compared to the loss that might be suffered by failing to make the diamond shift. To return a spade at trick two is equivalent to giving up.

There's More Than One Way to Skin a Cat

South dealer.
East-West vulnerable.

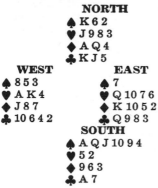

NORTH
♠ K 6 2
♥ J 9 8 3
♦ A Q 4
♣ K J 5

WEST
♠ 8 5 3
♥ A K 4
♦ J 8 7
♣ 10 6 4 2

EAST
♠ 7
♥ Q 10 7 6
♦ K 10 5 2
♣ Q 9 8 3

SOUTH
♠ A Q J 10 9 4
♥ 5 2
♦ 9 6 3
♣ A 7

The bidding:

South	West	North	East
1 ♠	Pass	2 NT	Pass
3 ♠	Pass	4 ♠	

Opening lead—king of hearts.

Card reading—the ability to deduce what cards the opponents have left, based on the bids and plays they have already made—is an important factor in the play of many hands.

Sometimes the declarer learns early in the play all he needs to know about the composition of the adverse hands. One simple clue may turn out to be the key to the entire hand. But you have to be alert to take advantage of the clue if you want to get the best possible result.

For example, take this deal. West leads the king of hearts, on which East signals with the seven. West continues with the ace and another heart, East covering the nine with the ten.

South ruffs, of course, but at the same time makes a mental note that East has the queen of hearts. Declarer doesn't actually see the queen, but he knows East has it. East's play of the 7-6-10 in that order would not make sense otherwise.

South also notes that the contract is in some danger. He has two diamond losers to take care of.

It may occur to him, after drawing three rounds of trumps, to lead the ace and another club and finesse the jack, hoping the finesse will win, in which case he would be home. And he may plan, at the same time, to fall back on a diamond finesse if the club jack loses to the queen.

However, despite the three-to-one probability that one finesse or the other will succeed, this would be the wrong line of play. The better method is to lead three rounds of trumps, ending in dummy, and then play the jack of hearts.

When East follows with the queen, South simply discards a diamond. This forces East to return either a diamond into the A-Q, or a club into the K-J.

This favorable position comes about because declarer locates the queen of hearts early in the play and applies that knowledge to construct a situation from which East cannot escape.

"What Can Beat Me?"

South dealer.
North-South vulnerable.

```
                NORTH
              ♠ Q J 7 3
              ♥ A 7 5
              ♦ K Q 8 6
              ♣ Q 2
   WEST                    EAST
♠ A 10 9 4              ♠ —
♥ 10 8 6 3             ♥ J 9 2
♦ 9 3                  ♦ 7 5 4 2
♣ J 8 6               ♣ 10 9 7 5 4 3
                SOUTH
              ♠ K 8 6 5 2
              ♥ K Q 4
              ♦ A J 10
              ♣ A K
```

The bidding:

South	West	North	East
1 ♠	Pass	3 ♠	Pass
4 NT	Pass	5 ♦	Pass
6 ♠			

Opening lead — three of hearts.

One trait that distinguishes the expert dummy player from the ordinary one is that he does not relax his vigil in the so-called easy hands. He always worries about the terrible things that might happen to him if the defenders' cards are badly divided.

Here is a hand where it would be easy for declarer to go wrong. A heart is led and South wins it with the king and leads a low spade. West plays low and dummy's jack wins, East showing out.

That is the end of the hand so far as South is concerned be-cause he must lose two trump tricks and go down one. He can attribute the result to bad luck if he wants to, but the fact is that he himself is responsible for the defeat.

The point is that South can see from the word go that the slam is sure to make if he loses only one trump trick. His tricks in the other three suits are solid. The only way he can lose two trump tricks is if the adverse spades are divided 4-0.

This division of the spades ordinarily occurs in only one deal out of ten, but there is no reason for South not to cater to this possibility. He should do everything he can to protect the contract.

He says to himself at trick one: "What can possibly beat me?" Since a 4-0 trump break is the outstanding danger, he does what he can to protect against it. He wins the heart in dummy and leads a low spade to the king.

When East shows out, it becomes a relatively simple matter for declarer to hold himself to one trump loser. West's 10-9-4 can be picked up by subsequent finesses.

It is true that the low spade play to the king will not succeed if East has the four trumps, but nothing can help declarer if this is the case. Leading the first spade from dummy provides protection against everything that can be protected against.

Performing
the
Impossible

South dealer.
Both sides vulnerable.

```
                NORTH
              ♠ A Q 6 5
              ♥ 8 7 3
              ♦ Q 3 2
              ♣ A 7 5
  WEST                   EAST
♠ 10 7 3              ♠ J 9 8 4
♥ A 10 2             ♥ K 9 6 4
♦ 5 4                ♦ 7
♣ K Q 10 8 6         ♣ J 4 3 2
                SOUTH
              ♠ K 2
              ♥ Q J 5
              ♦ A K J 10 9 8 6
              ♣ 9
```

The bidding:

South	West	North	East
1 ♦	Pass	1 ♠	Pass
3 ♦	Pass	6 ♦	

Opening lead—king of clubs.

You get to some contracts that are theoretically impossible to make, but, if you keep your cool, a surprising number of them will somehow or other come romping home.

Here is a good example of the art of performing the impossible. The hand appears in Dorothy Hayden's very excellent and newest book, *Winning Declarer Play.* South arrives at six diamonds on the bidding shown and West leads the king of clubs.

The slam looks hopeless, since there seems to be no way of avoiding two heart losers, but, as pointed out by Mrs. Hayden,

the picture is not altogether black. Declarer has a reasonable chance to make the contract if he can visualize a not-too-improbable distribution of the opponents' cards.

After winning the club lead with the ace, declarer plays a heart from dummy and puts up the queen after East follows low. West wins with the ace and can, of course, sink the contract by returning a heart at this point. But, lacking X-ray vision, he returns the queen of clubs, hoping that this will be the setting trick.

South ruffs and can no longer be defeated. He plays five rounds of trumps, producing this position:

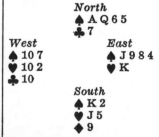

```
        North
      ♠ A Q 6 5
      ♣ 7
West              East
♠ 10 7            ♠ J 9 8 4
♥ 10 2            ♥ K
♣ 10
        South
      ♠ K 2
      ♥ J 5
      ♦ 9
```

When declarer now cashes his last trump, discarding a club from dummy, East finds he cannot afford to part with either a spade or a heart. Whatever he discards, South comes home with the seemingly impossible slam.

Never give up!

Signaling

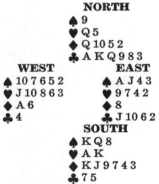

NORTH
♠ 9
♥ Q 5
♦ Q 10 5 2
♣ A K Q 9 8 3

WEST
♠ 10 7 6 5 2
♥ J 10 8 6 3
♦ A 6
♣ 4

EAST
♠ A J 4 3
♥ 9 7 4 2
♦ 8
♣ J 10 6 2

SOUTH
♠ K Q 8
♥ A K
♦ K J 9 7 4 3
♣ 7 5

The bidding:

North	East	South	West
1♣	Pass	1♦	Pass
2♦	Pass	4 NT	Pass
5♦			

Opening lead—four of clubs.

The suit-preference convention doesn't come up often, but when it does, it can be used with great effect.

For example, look at this deal where South was in five diamonds. South did well to stay out of a slam, considering that his partner had opened the bidding and raised diamonds immediately, but the Blackwood response of five diamonds, showing only one ace, put a quick end to South's ambitions.

West led a singleton club. East had no trouble diagnosing the lead as a singleton, not only because West had led dummy's suit, but also because the four

was the lowest club and would not have been led if West had held, say, the 7-4. (In that case, West would have opened the seven.)

Declarer played the queen from dummy and on it East played the jack. This was a signal designed to show that East had the ace of spades.

Accordingly, when declarer led a diamond from dummy at trick two, West took the ace and returned a spade. East won it with the ace, led a club, and South went down one.

It will be noted that without the use of the ruffing convention West would have had to guess whether to lead a spade or a heart after he had taken the ace of diamonds. If he had chosen a heart, South would have made the contract.

The convention is easy enough to use. When a ruff is about to take place, the play of an unnecessarily high card indicates an entry in the higher-ranking of the two side suits. (There are always only two suits to consider, since the trump suit and the suit to be ruffed do not count.)

In the same way, the play of a low card indicates an entry in the lower-ranking suit. Thus, in the present hand, if East had held the ace of hearts instead of the ace of spades, he would have played the two of clubs on the opening lead to guide his partner to the winning line of defense.

If
at First
You Don't Succeed . . .

South dealer.
Both sides vulnerable.

NORTH
♠ K J 6
♥ 9 2
♦ A Q 7 5 3
♣ J 10 9

WEST
♠ 8 7 5 2
♥ K J 3
♦ 10 8 6
♣ A K 6

EAST
♠ 4
♥ Q 10 6 5 4
♦ J 9 2
♣ Q 8 7 3

SOUTH
♠ A Q 10 9 3
♥ A 8 7
♦ K 4
♣ 5 4 2

The bidding:

South	West	North	East
1 ♠	Pass	2 ♦	Pass
2 ♠	Pass	4 ♠	

Opening lead—king of clubs.

Familiarity with how suits are likely to break is certainly helpful, but such knowledge is only one of many factors to be considered in the play of the cards.

South got to four spades and West led the king of clubs, East signaling with the eight. West continued with the ace and another club. East took the queen and returned a heart, declarer winning with the ace.

South had nine tricks in sight and the problem was to find the best way of winning the tenth. He knew that the prospect of finding a 3-3 diamond division was not good (only a 36% chance) and that the odds in favor of a 3-2 spade division were much better (68%).

So he cashed the king of diamonds, led a diamond to the queen, and ruffed a low diamond with the nine.

When he then played the ace of spades and continued with a spade to the king, East showed out and the hand collapsed. As a result, South went down two. Had the trumps been divided 3-2, he would have made the contract because he could then have cashed the jack of spades and discarded two hearts on the A-7 of diamonds.

Superficially, it would seem that South just had bad luck, but actually, he misplayed the hand.

What he should have done after taking the ace of hearts was first lead the ace and king of spades to see how the trumps were divided. If both defenders followed suit each time, proving that the spades were divided 3-2, he could then take two rounds of diamonds and ruff a diamond high. The jack of spades would provide the entry to utilize dummy's good diamonds.

But when, as in the actual case, he discovered a 4-1 division of the trumps, he would have had no alternative but to continue drawing trumps and play for a 3-3 diamond division.

By leading spades first, declarer would have given himself two chances to make the hand instead of just one.

Beginners' Luck

East dealer.
Neither side vulnerable.

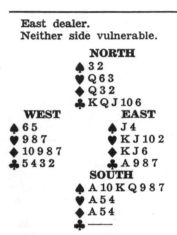

```
                    NORTH
                    ♠ 3 2
                    ♥ Q 6 3
                    ♦ Q 3 2
                    ♣ K Q J 10 6
    WEST                          EAST
    ♠ 6 5                         ♠ J 4
    ♥ 9 8 7                       ♥ K J 10 2
    ♦ 10 9 8 7                    ♦ K J 6
    ♣ 5 4 3 2                     ♣ A 9 8 7
                    SOUTH
                    ♠ A 10 K Q 9 8 7
                    ♥ A 5 4
                    ♦ A 5 4
                    ♣ —
```

The bidding:

East	South	West	North
1♣	2♣	Pass	3 NT
Pass	6♠		

Opening lead—two of clubs.

Pinochle is a crazy, mixed-up game—at least to anyone not familiar with it. Not only are there 48 cards in the deck instead of 52, but there are also no cards lower than a nine.

What's more, there are two queens of spades in the deck, two aces of hearts, and, in fact, every card has a twin—an identical twin, no less.

Just to add to the confusion, the cards rank in order from the ace down to the nine, just as in bridge, but for one exception—the ten is higher than the king!

Now my friend John, an inveterate pinochle player who never said a kind word about bridge in all his years—though he understood the game—was in the club one day and there weren't enough players around to form a pinochle game. So he consented to play bridge just for kicks.

The first hand out of the box he picked up the South duke. He quickly got to six spades. Now John is a pretty good card player, and saw right away that he couldn't make twelve tricks even though he got a club lead and ruffed the ace.

But he thought that if he ran off all the trumps the defense might get mixed up and chuck the hand to him. So he led the ace of spades, continued with the ten, and was just about to play the king when East interrupted and said, "It's my lead."

You see, John had forgotten he was playing bridge, not pinochle, and that the ten did not rank next to the ace. So East won the ten with the jack.

But this inadvertent play turned out to be just what the doctor ordered. East was on lead and had to return a club or else play away from one of his red kings. As a result of the goof, John made the slam.

John doesn't play pinochle any more. You just can't tear him away from the bridge table.

Watching
for the Clues

West dealer.
East-West vulnerable.

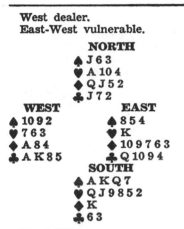

NORTH
♠ J 6 3
♥ A 10 4
♦ Q J 5 2
♣ J 7 2

WEST
♠ 10 9 2
♥ 7 6 3
♦ A 8 4
♣ A K 8 5

EAST
♠ 8 5 4
♥ K
♦ 10 9 7 6 3
♣ Q 10 9 4

SOUTH
♠ A K Q 7
♥ Q J 9 8 5 2
♦ K
♣ 6 3

The bidding:

West	North	East	South
Pass	Pass	Pass	1 ♥
Pass	2 ♥	Pass	4 ♥

Opening lead—king of clubs.

You sometimes hear that a certain expert made a certain play in a certain hand and that the play, startling though it was, turned out to be sensationally correct.

The feeling you get is something like the one you have while watching a magician perform a skillful trick. You see it done, and though you can't understand how or why it works, the fact remains that the trick was performed right before your eyes.

The big difference between bridge and magic is that there is nothing really mysterious about these striking plays in bridge. There is practically always a sound and sensible explanation for a good play at bridge.

Take this hand, for example. South got to four hearts and West led the king of clubs, East signaling with the ten. West cashed the ace and then led another club, which declarer ruffed.

South now played the king of diamonds. West grabbed the ace and shifted to the ten of spades. Declarer won it in his hand and led the queen of hearts. West followed low and declarer, spurning the finesse, went up with the ace, caught the king, and easily took the rest of the tricks.

Now how did South know the king was going to fall? The answer is that he didn't. Then how come he refused the finesse? Did this play, decidedly contrary to normal percentage, have some reason behind it, or was it just a lucky stab?

Well, let's say right away it wasn't just luck. There was more to it than that. South had paid close attention to the bidding and he applied this knowledge to take advantage of the situation. He had seen West show up with the A-K of clubs and ace of diamonds during the play. He had heard West pass originally and also at his next opportunity.

He therefore knew that West could not have the king of hearts. So rather than take a finesse sure to lose, he went up with the ace on the off chance that the king was alone.

31

The Impossible Takes a Little Longer

South dealer.
Both sides vulnerable.

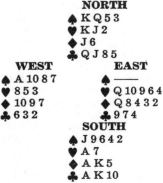

NORTH
♠ K Q 5 3
♥ K J 2
♦ J 6
♣ Q J 8 5

WEST
♠ A 10 8 7
♥ 8 5 3
♦ 10 9 7
♣ 6 3 2

EAST
♠ —
♥ Q 10 9 6 4
♦ Q 8 4 3 2
♣ 9 7 4

SOUTH
♠ J 9 6 4 2
♥ A 7
♦ A K 5
♣ A K 10

The bidding:

South	West	North	East
1 ♠	Pass	3 ♠	Pass
6 ♠			

Opening lead—ten of diamonds.

Doing the impossible is a sort of contradiction in terms, but there are situations in bridge where what appears to be impossible · can be accomplished nevertheless.

For example, look at this hand. South arrives at a contract of six spades, reached in an entirely reasonable manner.

South would ordinarily encounter no trouble making the contract, but in this case he has his hands full because West has all four missing trumps.

Suspecting nothing out of the ordinary, declarer wins the diamond lead with the ace and plays a low spade. West follows with the seven, dummy plays the queen, and East shows out.

It now appears that West has two sure trump tricks. Apparently, all he has to do is sit and wait for them. But if declarer pays attention to his knitting, West winds up with only one trump trick.

South's only hope is to arrange a trump endplay. This can be successfully accomplished if West has the right distribution in the three side suits.

Accordingly, South cashes the ace and king of hearts and trumps the jack; then he cashes the king of diamonds and trumps a diamond; and next he cashes the A-K-Q of clubs to bring about this position:

North
♠ K 5
♣ J

West
♠ A 10 8

East
Immaterial

South
♠ J 9 6

The lead is in dummy and the jack of clubs is played, South ruffing with the jack.

What can West do? If he overruffs with the ace, he is on lead, and whether he returns the eight or the ten, declarer makes the last two tricks.

West is likewise in trouble if he underruffs the jack. South simply plays a spade towards dummy and West scores only the ace.

It just goes to show that, no matter how tough the going sometimes is, you don't give up.

Bridge
Is a Strange
Game

West dealer.
Both sides vulnerable.

NORTH
♠ 10 9 5
♥ 10
♦ 10
♣ A K Q J 8 6 5 2

WEST
♠ K J 7 6
♥ A K Q 9 6 4
♦ 8 7
♣ 9

EAST
♠ A 8 4 2
♥ 7 3
♦ 9 6 5 3 2
♣ 4 3

SOUTH
♠ Q 3
♥ J 8 5 2
♦ A K Q J 4
♣ 10 7

The bidding:

West	North	East	South
1 ♥	3 ♣	Pass	3 NT

Opening lead—king of hearts.

This deal occurred in a pair championship. The bidding was not the same at every table, but at most of them South became declarer at three notrump.

The results obtained by the various declarers were curious indeed. The outcome was largely a matter of West's choosing the right line of defense, and we record here what transpired at three tables where South contracted for three notrump.

At the first table, West led the king of hearts and was then faced with a difficult choice of what to play next. With eight solid clubs staring him in the face, West decided that the best chance of beating the contract was to play his partner for the ace of diamonds.

So at trick two he led a diamond in the hope that East would take the ace and return a heart to defeat the contract three tricks. This scheme didn't turn out well for West, because South, to West's discomfiture, took the rest of the tricks to make six notrump.

At the second table, West cashed the A-K-Q of hearts, and when East signaled on the third heart lead with the eight of spades, West led the six. East took the ace, returned a spade, and West cashed three spades to defeat the contract three tricks.

It was at the third table that the defense exacted the maximum penalty. Here, also, the king of hearts was led, but at trick two West shifted to a low spade. East won with the ace and returned a heart.

Declarer, who had thirteen tricks ready to cash if he could have obtained the lead in time, sat by hopelessly as the defenders reeled off six heart tricks and four spades to defeat him six tricks—600 points.

So the odd result of the hand was that while all three declarers were playing the same contract against the same opening lead, one of them made twelve tricks, another six tricks, and the third one made only three tricks.

Bridge is a strange game.

You Can't Win 'Em All

South dealer.
North-South vulnerable.

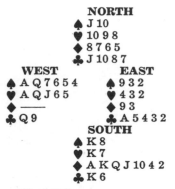

```
              NORTH
            ♠ J 10
            ♥ 10 9 8
            ♦ 8 7 6 5
            ♣ J 10 8 7
  WEST                    EAST
♠ A Q 7 6 5 4          ♠ 9 3 2
♥ A Q J 6 5            ♥ 4 3 2
♦ ——                   ♦ 9 3
♣ Q 9                  ♣ A 5 4 3 2
              SOUTH
            ♠ K 8
            ♥ K 7
            ♦ A K Q J 10 4 2
            ♣ K 6
```

The bidding:

South	West	North	East
1 ♦	1 ♠	Pass	Pass
1 NT	2 ♥	Pass	Pass
2 NT	Dble	Pass	Pass
Redble			

Martin Cohn, well-known Atlanta expert, tells this story about himself, and quite a story it is. He was South and the bidding went as shown.

Had West led a spade or a heart, Cohn would have made the contract. But West, apparently suspecting the type of hand he was competing against, led the nine of clubs instead. This proved to be an exceptionally effective lead when East won with the ace and returned the deuce of spades.

Declarer followed low, hoping against hope that East had the queen. But West showed up with the damsel and cashed the ace, East following suit with the three and thus blocking the suit.

However, the block proved to be no hardship to the defense when West continued with a spade to East's nine. East returned a heart, trapping South's king and allowing West to cash five hearts as well as his three remaining spades.

By this time twelve tricks had been played and East-West had won them all. Cohn was already down seven—4,000 points —with one trick to go.

Perhaps the story should end right here, but actually South's agony was not yet over. When West cashed his twelfth trick, Cohn still had a discard to choose. His last two cards were the king of clubs and ace of diamonds—and he had to guess which one to discard.

Unfortunately, he decided to discard the king of clubs, since he could not tell whether West's last card was a diamond or a club. West thereupon cashed the queen of clubs and the extraordinary outcome was that South went down eight—4,600 points. He failed to score a trick.

Obviously Cohn misplayed the hand. He should have held the loss to 4,000 points!

A Little Learning Is a Dangerous Thing

East dealer.
Neither side vulnerable.

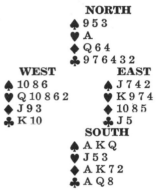

NORTH
♠ 9 5 3
♥ A
♦ Q 6 4
♣ 9 7 6 4 3 2

WEST
♠ 10 8 6
♥ Q 10 8 6 2
♦ J 9 3
♣ K 10

EAST
♠ J 7 4 2
♥ K 9 7 4
♦ 10 8 5
♣ J 5

SOUTH
♠ A K Q
♥ J 5 3
♦ A K 7 2
♣ A Q 8

The bidding:

East	South	West	North
Pass	2 NT	Pass	3 NT

Opening lead—six of hearts.

When a contract depends on how the opponents' cards are divided, declarer cannot do better than follow the indicated probabilities.

This question of percentages is sometimes simple and sometimes complicated, but unless you're an expert mathematician, you will run into many problems that are difficult to solve. Fortunately, most hands don't present such headaches and most of the percentage plays that do arise can be worked out on a common sense basis.

Look at this hand where South was in three notrump. He won the heart lead in dummy and saw that he had eight sure tricks. He knew that the ninth trick could come from a successful club finesse, and he also knew that the ninth trick could be taken in diamonds if that suit was divided 3-3.

South knew enough about probabilities to realize he had a 50% chance of winning the club finesse and only a 36% chance of finding an even division of the diamonds. So at trick two he led a club and finessed. West took the queen with the king and continued hearts and South went down one.

He should have made the contract, of course. It was a case of misapplied knowledge. South's statistics were correct as far as he went, but he didn't go far enough.

After winning the ace of hearts, South should have cashed the A-K of diamonds and then led a diamond to the queen. In the actual case, he would have discovered the 3-3 diamond division and his worries would have been over. He could cash nine tricks quickly and not bother with the club finesse.

Let's suppose, though, that the diamonds had not been divided 3-3, which he would have found out when one opponent failed to follow suit. He could then fall back on the club finesse and hope for the best.

This method of play would have given him two chances to make the hand instead of one, and would have raised his prospects of success well beyond 50%.

A Machiavellian Play

South dealer.
East-West vulnerable.

```
                    NORTH
                 ♠ A Q J 9
                 ♥ Q J 6 3
                 ♦ 7 3
                 ♣ J 10 4
     WEST                        EAST
  ♠ 7 4 3                     ♠ K 6
  ♥ 5 4                       ♥ K 2
  ♦ 10 8 6 2                  ♦ A K Q 9 5
  ♣ 9 8 5 3                   ♣ Q 7 6 2
                    SOUTH
                 ♠ 10 8 5 2
                 ♥ A 10 9 8 7
                 ♦ J 4
                 ♣ A K
```

The bidding:

South	West	North	East
1 ♥	Pass	1 ♠	2 ♦
2 ♠	Pass	4 ♥	

Opening lead—two of diamonds.

To know what the other fellow has and what he is thinking. and then put it to advantage, is the mark of a really good player. You have to put yourself in the other fellow's shoes to get the best result in some hands.

This hand is an exercise in card reading and psychology. Suppose you're sitting East, defending against four hearts. West leads a diamond and you take two diamond tricks. What would you lead now?

When the hand was played, East returned the six of spades! As a result of this play, he defeated the contract.

Of course, South could have made five hearts once the spade was led, and anyone reading this column would surely make eleven tricks—*provided he saw the East-West hands.* But to understand why declarer went down, you have to imagine you're South and see only the North-South hands.

From South's viewpoint, the spade play at trick three has all the earmarks of a singleton. Why else would East lead a spade when he has such a natural club return?

So when you win the spade in dummy and lead the queen of hearts and East follows low, it seems foolish to finesse because, if West has the king, he'll take it and give partner a spade ruff to defeat the contract.

You therefore go up with the ace of hearts and return a heart. East takes it and leads a club. You win and confidently take the spade finesse, but East, the rascal, produces the king and down you go. If you're not too upset by what East did to you, you congratulate him for a fine play.

East's spade return makes lots of sense when you think of it. He knows South must have the A-K of clubs for his opening bid and rebid, and that a club return is futile. If South is left to his own devices, he is sure to take a spade finesse and a heart finesse and make the hand.

East therefore throws a monkey-wrench into the works by returning a spade.

How to Succeed
Without
Even Trying

South dealer.
Both sides vulnerable.

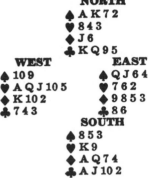

NORTH
♠ A K 7 2
♥ 8 4 3
♦ J 6
♣ K Q 9 5

WEST
♠ 10 9
♥ A Q J 10 5
♦ K 10 2
♣ 7 4 3

EAST
♠ Q J 6 4
♥ 7 6 2
♦ 9 8 5 3
♣ 8 6

SOUTH
♠ 8 5 3
♥ K 9
♦ A Q 7 4
♣ A J 10 2

The bidding:

South	West	North	East
1 ♦	1 ♥	1 ♠	Pass
1 NT	Pass	3 NT	

Opening lead—ten of spades.

Suppose you became declarer at three notrump and West, who overcalled in hearts, leads the ten of spades. As usual in notrump contracts, you would start by counting sure winners.

The count reveals seven quick tricks. Since your goal is nine tricks, you start by looking for the line of play with the best chance of acquiring two more tricks.

There are several clues available concerning the likely disposition of the adverse high cards. One thing fairly certain is that your king of hearts isn't worth much if East ever gets on lead to play through it. West is marked by the bidding to have the ace of hearts.

Another important card missing is the king of diamonds. You can't be positive that West has it, but you say to yourself that he is far more likely to have the king than East.

It does you no good to lead the jack of diamonds from dummy and take a finesse, because if East has the king he will cover the jack, while if West has the king, he will win the jack—and in either case, all you will have done is acquire an eighth trick with not much hope of a ninth.

No, the best thing to do is to hope that West has the king and play accordingly. Therefore, after winning the spade lead with the king, you cross to your hand with a club and play a low diamond towards the jack.

If West goes up with the king, you've got the hand made. That would give you three diamond tricks instead of the one you started with. So let's assume West lets you win the diamond with the jack.

Now you cash three more club tricks and the ace of spades and lead a diamond to the ace. Then you exit with a diamond in order to saddle West with the lead. He is forced to return a heart to your king, and, in that way, you make the contract.

Time
Is of
the Essence

East dealer.
East-West vulnerable.

```
                NORTH
              ♠ Q
              ♥ 9 8 6 2
              ♦ K 8 3
              ♣ K Q J 9 4
   WEST                    EAST
♠ K 5 3 2               ♠ A J 10 7 4
♥ 7 5                   ♥ A 3
♦ 9 7 4                 ♦ Q J 10 6
♣ 8 7 6 3              ♣ A 2
                SOUTH
              ♠ 9 8 6
              ♥ K Q J 10 4
              ♦ A 5 2
              ♣ 10 5
```

The bidding:

East	South	West	North
1 ♠	2 ♥	Pass	4 ♥

Opening lead—two of spades.

In every hand declarer plays in a suit contract he is faced with the problem of whether or not to draw trumps. There is no accurate general rule to guide him to when to tackle trumps and when not to. The declarer can solve this problem only by weighing the factors that prevail in the particular hand he is playing.

One of the most important of these factors is timing. The order in which various plays are made may prove to be decisive. For example, study this hand where South is in four hearts and West leads a spade. East takes the ace and returns the queen of diamonds.

South is faced with the problem of avoiding a loser in each of the four suits. He cannot afford to tackle trumps at once because the defense would take the ace and lead another diamond, which would establish the setting trick and lead to sure defeat.

So South wins the queen of diamonds with the ace and leads the ten of clubs. He wants to set up the clubs in dummy so that he can obtain a valuable discard of a diamond on one of the clubs. If he saves the diamond loser, he makes the contract.

Let's say East ducks the ten but then wins the next club with the ace. He returns the jack of diamonds, taken in dummy with the king.

Declarer now leads a high club, hoping the suit is divided 3-3 and that he will be able to discard his diamond loser. But East ruffs with a low trump and South has to overruff to escape immediate defeat.

South then trumps a spade in dummy and leads still another club. This time the club lead is successful. East is faced with an impossible choice. If he ruffs with the ace, South sheds his diamond, thus telescoping two losers into one. And if East discards on the club instead, South disposes of his diamond loser and then loses only a trump trick, thus making the contract.

A
Little Less
Bidding Please

South dealer.
Both sides vulnerable.

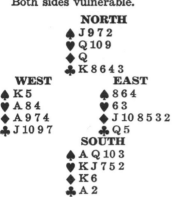

NORTH
♠ J 9 7 2
♥ Q 10 9
♦ Q
♣ K 8 6 4 3

WEST
♠ K 5
♥ A 8 4
♦ A 9 7 4
♣ J 10 9 7

EAST
♠ 8 6 4
♥ 6 3
♦ J 10 8 5 3 2
♣ Q 5

SOUTH
♠ A Q 10 3
♥ K J 7 5 2
♦ K 6
♣ A 2

The bidding:

South	West	North	East
1 ♥	Pass	2 ♥	Pass
2 ♠	Pass	3 ♠	Pass
4 ♠			

Good bidding should get you to the best contract practically all the time. Each bid made sends a message which partner interprets and to which he replies in turn so that a maximum amount of information is exchanged.

Eventually, after the messages have shuttled back and forth for a while, a final contract is reached for better or worse.

For example, when South opens the bidding with a heart, he is saying he has an opening bid, though how strong or weak it is in high cards or distribution is not known at once.

When North responds two hearts, he sends a fairly exact message. He states he has from 6 to 9 points including heart support.

When South bids again, he shows values beyond a minimum opening bid; otherwise he would be expected to pass. The two spade bid furthermore proposes a different suit as trump and asks partner to choose between hearts and spades.

The raise to three spades guarantees four-card support and shows willingness to go along with South's advance towards game. The four spade bid closes the auction.

There is one serious drawback to such lengthy exchanges of information. While the partners are busy sending messages across the table for their own edification, the opponents can't help listening in. What they overhear frequently enables them to find the best line of defense.

West took advantage of the bidding in this deal to find the killing lead. He began with the ace and another heart, and there was then no way for declarer to prevent West from giving East a heart ruff to defeat the contract a trick.

West decided, reasonably enough, that North-South were bound to have at least eight hearts between them for the heart bid and raise. This meant that East would have at most two hearts and that a ruff was therefore possible either immediately or eventually.

If South had been less scientific during the bidding, and jumped directly to four hearts, he could not have been beaten.

Keeping in Touch

South dealer.
North-South vulnerable.

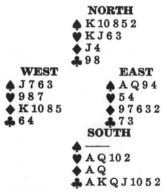

```
                  NORTH
                ♠ K 10 8 5 2
                ♥ K J 6 3
                ♦ J 4
                ♣ 9 8
   WEST                       EAST
 ♠ J 7 6 3                  ♠ A Q 9 4
 ♥ 9 8 7                    ♥ 5 4
 ♦ K 10 8 5                 ♦ 9 7 6 3 2
 ♣ 6 4                      ♣ 7 3
                  SOUTH
                ♠ ——
                ♥ A Q 10 2
                ♦ A Q
                ♣ A K Q J 10 5 2
```

The bidding:

South	West	North	East
2 ♣	Pass	2 ♠	Pass
3 ♣	Pass	3 ♥	Pass
7 ♣			

Opening lead—nine of hearts.

The problem of entries plagues the declarer in the play of many hands. Insufficient communication between one hand and the other will often break a contract that could otherwise be made. It follows that in hands where the communication lines appear outwardly inadequate, declarer should do everything possible to create additional entries to the hand that needs them.

Look at this hand, for example, where South is in seven clubs. A superficial glance might indicate that declarer needs a successful diamond finesse to make the contract. However, a little study will show that it is possible for the hand to be made if the East-West cards are favorably divided, even though the diamond finesse, if attempted, would fail.

Declarer therefore plans from the beginning to exhaust all other possibilities before committing the outcome of the hand to the success of the diamond finesse.

Accordingly, he wins the heart lead with the jack, being careful to drop the ten from his hand. He then ruffs a low spade with the ten. He crosses to the eight of clubs and ruffs a low spade with the jack. He next plays a club to the nine and ruffs the third round of spades.

The purpose of these ruffs is to try to drop the ace of spades as the suit is being ruffed. If the ace were to fall on the first, second, or third spade lead, a diamond finesse would become unnecessary.

Now declarer cashes the ace of hearts, both defenders following suit, and leads the queen, overtaking with the king. He then plays the ten of spades, finally bringing about the fall of the ace.

The deuce of hearts, carefully preserved, provides an entry to dummy's six, and the queen of diamonds is discarded on the king of spades.

Note that the diamond finesse was held in reserve in case the spades broke unfavorably, and note also that dropping the ten of hearts on the jack was necessary in order to provide an extra entry to dummy.

Courage
or Foolhardiness?

South dealer.
North-South vulnerable.

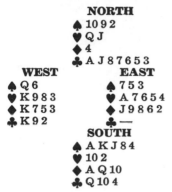

NORTH
♠ 10 9 2
♥ Q J
♦ 4
♣ A J 8 7 6 5 3

WEST
♠ Q 6
♥ K 9 8 3
♦ K 7 5 3
♣ K 9 2

EAST
♠ 7 5 3
♥ A 7 6 5 4
♦ J 9 8 6 2
♣ —

SOUTH
♠ A K J 8 4
♥ 10 2
♦ A Q 10
♣ Q 10 4

The bidding:

South	West	North	East
1 ♠	Pass	2 ♣	Pass
3 ♠	Pass	4 ♠	Dble.
Pass	Pass	Redble.	

Courage is a valuable commodity at the bridge table, but where courage ends and foolhardiness begins is a matter each one has to judge for himself.

You can't say that the East in this hand lacked either fortitude or imagination when he doubled four spades. Certainly, he didn't have four defensive tricks to point to, but yet, his double was not as farfetched as first appears.

East thought that his double against the strong bidding put up by North-South would necessarily be interpreted by West as lead-directing. He reasoned that if West had a trick the contract would be defeated with a club lead.

He would ruff the opening club, put his partner back in the lead for another club ruff, and thus defeat the contract with the aid of his ace of hearts. And, as a matter of fact, that is more or less what would have happened if West had led a club and declarer finessed. East would have ruffed, played the ace and another heart, and gotten another ruff.

But West didn't quite appreciate what was going on. He failed to read the double as lead-directing. He opened a low heart which East took with the ace. East returned a heart to the king and now, catching on at last, West led the nine of clubs.

Declarer, afraid this was a singleton, went up with the ace only to have it ruffed. East led back a trump and declarer, completely confused, finessed. West won with the queen, cashed the king of clubs, played another club for East to trump, and that was the end of the party. Down 1,600.

Of course, South would have been better off if he had finessed the club at trick three instead of going up with the ace. In fact, he would have been 2,830 points better off. He could have been plus 1,230 instead of minus 1,600.

Did East make a bad double? Did West make a bad lead? It all depends on how you look at it. If you think pragmatically, East-West played perfectly.

An Elegant Play

South dealer.
Both sides vulnerable.

```
                NORTH
              ♠ J 5 4
              ♥ Q 10 7 6
              ♦ A
              ♣ A K J 10 3
   WEST                    EAST
 ♠ 3                     ♠ Q 9 8 7
 ♥ K 8 4                 ♥ J 5 2
 ♦ J 9 6 5 2             ♦ K 7 4 3
 ♣ 9 7 6 2               ♣ 8 4
                SOUTH
              ♠ A K 10 6 2
              ♥ A 9 3
              ♦ Q 10 8
              ♣ Q 5
```

The bidding:

South	West	North	East
1 ♠	Pass	2 ♣	Pass
2 NT	Pass	3 ♠	Pass
4 ♠	Pass	6 ♠	

Opening lead—five of diamonds.

Let's say you are the declarer at six spades and West leads a diamond. How would you go about playing the hand?

It is not an easy hand to play correctly if you do not see the opponents' cards, and, as a matter of fact, it is somewhat difficult to make the contract even if you do see them. If you'd like to exercise your skill before reading on, go right ahead and enjoy yourself.

Suppose you win the diamond with the ace and lead a low spade and finesse the ten. The finesse would win in the actual hand and you could then ruff a diamond in dummy and play another spade, hoping for a 3-2 spade break, in which case you would make all the tricks.

But when West shows out, your house of cards collapses. No matter which way you turn, you are bound to go down. The 4-1 trump break defeats you.

Now what you should do in this type of hand is try to protect against a 4-1 trump break. After all, this is not rare, since such a division occurs in more than a quarter of all deals.

The proper way to play the hand is to lead the jack of spades at trick two and duck it. It does not matter that East covers the jack with the queen —you still duck.

Once you make this play and West follows suit, you stop worrying about the hand. What East returns is of no great consequence.

Suppose East leads back a spade. You win it, ruff a diamond in dummy, return to your hand with a heart or a club, draw trumps, and claim the rest.

Suppose East returns a heart. You go up with the ace, ruff a diamond, draw trumps, and again make twelve tricks.

Either way, you make four trump tricks, a heart, a diamond, a diamond ruff, and five clubs. All of this comes about because you are realistic enough to guard against a possible 4-1 trump division.

A
Change
of Heart

South dealer.
North-South vulnerable.

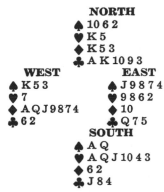

NORTH
♠ 10 6 2
♥ K 5
♦ K 5 3
♣ A K 10 9 3

WEST
♠ K 5 3
♥ 7
♦ A Q J 9 8 7 4
♣ 6 2

EAST
♠ J 9 8 7 4
♥ 9 8 6 2
♦ 10
♣ Q 7 5

SOUTH
♠ A Q
♥ A Q J 10 4 3
♦ 6 2
♣ J 8 4

The bidding:

South	West	North	East
1♥	4♦	4♥	Pass
Pass	Pass		

Opening lead—ace of diamonds.

This hand, reported in *The Bridge World* magazine, occurred in a tournament. North had a difficult choice of bids to make over four diamonds and decided in favor of four hearts, despite his holding of only two trumps. He didn't like the idea of being talked out of a vulnerable game.

West led the ace of diamonds and continued with the queen. Declarer played the king from dummy and East ruffed. East returned a spade. Declarer finessed, losing the queen to the king. It was the third trick for the defense. South later attempted a club finesse, which also lost, and the result was that South ended going down one.

North was properly sympathetic. "There wasn't anything you could do about it," he said. "You lost two finesses, East had to have a singleton diamond, and besides, West had to find the diamond lead to beat the hand.

"I guess I should have doubled four diamonds. We would have gotten them for three tricks."

When North had finished, East delicately pointed out that South could have made the contract. He said South should have ducked the queen of diamonds at trick two, since it was obvious on the bidding that East would trump the king if it was played.

The defense would then be unable to stop the contract. If East discarded on the queen and West continued with a diamond, East could ruff, but declarer would overruff, draw trumps, and finesse the club to make the hand. His spade queen would go on dummy's fourth club.

Nor would it help East to trump the queen of diamonds, because declarer, in that case, would be able to discard the queen of spades on the king of diamonds. South would lose two diamonds and a club on this line of defense.

North had listened closely to East's analysis of the play, which was obviously correct, and when East was all through, he turned to South and snapped, "Well, why didn't you play it that way?"

Sylvia
Invents
a New Play

East dealer.
Both sides vulnerable.

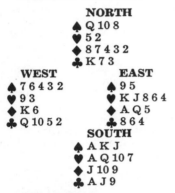

NORTH
♠ Q 10 8
♥ 5 2
♦ 8 7 4 3 2
♣ K 7 3

WEST
♠ 7 6 4 3 2
♥ 9 3
♦ K 6
♣ Q 10 5 2

EAST
♠ 9 5
♥ K J 8 6 4
♦ A Q 5
♣ 8 6 4

SOUTH
♠ A K J
♥ A Q 10 7
♦ J 10 9
♣ A J 9

The bidding:

East	South	West	North
Pass	2 NT	Pass	3 NT

Opening lead—nine of hearts.

Perhaps the most striking aspect of Sylvia's game was that so many of her triumphs were the result of some gross misconception of a principle she supposedly had assimilated.

Sylvia never intentionally varied from what she understood to be the correct bid or play. As a matter of fact, she would almost woodenly follow her partner's suggestions, even though it seemed to her that many of the principles they vociferously espoused were in total conflict with one another.

One day, Sylvia was playing as usual in the expert game at the club and became declarer at three notrump with the South hand.

West had no really clear-cut opening lead, and chose the nine of hearts in an effort to find his partner's long suit.

East signaled enthusiastic approval with the six, but Sylvia, who had been told time and again of the virtues and advantages of the hold-up play at trick one, followed suit with the seven!

This extraordinary play was but one more example of the lengths to which Sylvia would go to please her partners.

West continued with a heart and Sylvia captured East's eight with the ten. When she now led the jack of diamonds, West won with the king and, unable to return a heart, shifted to a low spade. Sylvia won with the ace and led another diamond. East took the queen, but was absolutely helpless. A heart return was obviously futile, since Sylvia still had the A-Q, so East returned a spade.

Sylvia won and played still another diamond, finally establishing dummy's long suit to produce nine tricks.

Later analysis revealed that Sylvia would have gone down had she won the opening heart lead with the ten. East's hearts would have become established before Sylvia's diamonds, and the contract would inevitably have failed.

Laying
a
Trap

North dealer.
Neither side vulnerable.

NORTH
♠ A 10
♥ 10 4 3
♦ A 8 7 6
♣ A 10 9 2

WEST
♠ Q J 9 6
♥ K
♦ J 9 4 2
♣ J 6 5 3

EAST
♠ 8 7 5 3
♥ Q J 9 6
♦ 10 5
♣ K 8 7

SOUTH
♠ K 4 2
♥ A 8 7 5 2
♦ K Q 3
♣ Q 4

The bidding:

North	East	South	West
1 ♦	Pass	1 ♥	Pass
1 NT	Pass	3 ♦	Pass
3 ♥	Pass	4 ♥	

Opening lead — queen of spades.

A fine declarer makes not only the tricks he's supposed to make, but also some he's not supposed to make. These added tricks are frequently the result of a deliberate effort by him to induce a mistake by the defense.

Here is an example of such a case. South is declarer at four hearts and West leads the queen of spades. As can be seen by looking at all four hands, South should go down one. The trumps break badly and he should lose three hearts and a club.

But if declarer is on his toes, there is a good chance he will make the contract. While he does not see the opponents' cards, and therefore does not know that the trumps are divided 4-1, he plans his play on the basis that that is the case.

He realizes that a 3-2 trump break will automatically give him the contract, so he tries to take whatever steps he can to guard against a 4-1 division. He therefore wins the spade in dummy with the ace and leads the ten of hearts.

Now put yourself in the East position, imagining that you see only the dummy's hand and your own. How many players do you know who would play the six when the ten is led?

The fact is that nearly everybody would cover the ten with the jack, and no sooner would this take place than declarer would make the hand. He would play the ace, catching the king, cash the king of spades and ruff a spade, and then lead a heart from dummy. East would win two trump tricks and a club, but South would make the contract.

Note that if declarer's first trump lead from dummy is a low one instead of the ten, it would be normal for East also to play low. South would eventually lose three trump tricks and go down as a result of his failure to give East a chance to make a mistake.

Revelation

North dealer.
East-West vulnerable.

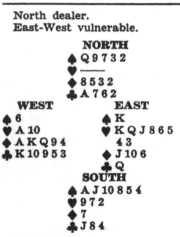

```
                    NORTH
                 ♠ Q 9 7 3 2
                 ♥ —
                 ♦ 8 5 3 2
                 ♣ A 7 6 2
      WEST                    EAST
   ♠ 6                     ♠ K
   ♥ A 10                  ♥ K Q J 8 6 5
   ♦ A K Q 9 4            ♦ 4 3
   ♣ K 10 9 5 3           ♦ J 10 6
                          ♣ Q
                    SOUTH
                 ♠ A J 10 8 5 4
                 ♥ 9 7 2
                 ♦ 7
                 ♣ J 8 4
```

The bidding:

North	East	South	West
Pass	1 ♥	1 ♠	2 ♦
2 ♠	4 ♥	Pass	Pass
4 ♠	5 ♥	Pass	Pass
5 ♠	Pass	Pass	Dble.

Opening lead—king of diamonds.

The ability to count out a hand is the greatest single asset in the declarer's bag of tricks. Counting is not really a difficult process—you never go beyond the number 13—but the fact is that most players are inclined to be lazy when it comes to counting a hand. They seem to look upon it as something beyond their reach.

Yet, see how easy (or difficult) it is in this hand where South is in five spades doubled. You may not agree with the bidding, but that's the way it went.

West led the king of dia-

monds and continued with the ace. Declarer ruffed and cashed the ace of spades, felling the king. In alternating order, he then trumped three hearts in dummy and two diamonds in his hand, ending in dummy after the last ruff.

By this time, dummy consisted of one trump and four clubs, while South had two trumps and three clubs. Then came the crucial play—a low club from dummy. East won with the queen, and having only hearts left, was forced to lead one.

This permitted South to dispose of his club loser as the heart was ruffed in dummy, and he made five spades doubled.

Note that if South had led the ace and another club at the crucial point, he would have gone down one.

The particular South in this case was well versed in the art of counting. He knew that East had started with *one* spade. He knew that East had started with *eight* hearts (since West had shown out on the third lead of hearts). He knew that East had started with *three* diamonds (having shown out on the fourth lead of the suit).

With twelve of East's cards exactly accounted for, it was certain that East had started with one club. The low club play was made in the hope that East had the singleton K, Q or 10, in all of which cases one defender or the other would have to commit hara-kiri on the next lead.

46

Dummy Reversal

South dealer.
North-South vulnerable.

NORTH
♠ A J 5
♥ K 10 9
♦ K 6 2
♣ K 8 7 3

WEST
♠ 9 7 2
♥ 8 5 3
♦ J 10 8 5
♣ Q 10 6

EAST
♠ 8 6 3
♥ 7 4
♦ Q 7 4
♣ A J 9 4 2

SOUTH
♠ K Q 10 4
♥ A Q J 6 2
♦ A 9 3
♣ 5

The bidding:

South	West	North	East
1 ♥	Pass	2 NT	Pass
3 ♠	Pass	4 ♥	Pass
4 NT	Pass	5 ♦	Pass
6 ♥			

Opening lead — jack of diamonds.

One play frequently overlooked is the one known as "dummy reversal." It is actually not a difficult play to execute; the reason it is missed so often is that declarer simply does not see it.

South is in six hearts and West leads a diamond. Declarer takes it with the ace and leads a club. He hopes that West has the ace, in which case he will be able to discard his diamond loser on the king.

However, the king loses to the ace and East returns a diamond. (No other play by East would matter.) Declarer wins the return with the king and now embarks on a dummy reversal. Instead of drawing trumps at this point, which would seem to be natural, he ruffs a club.

He then plays a heart to the nine and trumps another club with the jack. After entering dummy with a heart to the king, he then ruffs the last club with his last trump, the ace.

The effect of these plays is that he has ruffed three of dummy's clubs in his hand, and, in the process of going back and forth, he has also extracted all but one of the outstanding trumps.

South now plays a spade to the ace and cashes the ten of hearts, drawing West's eight at the same time as he disposes of the nine of diamonds. Declarer's last three cards are the K-Q-10 of spades, which he cashes to make the contract.

When the play is examined, it is found that South made twelve tricks, consisting of four spades, six hearts and two diamonds. When the play started, he had only eleven tricks, consisting of four spades, five hearts and two diamonds.

The trick gained came from what is known as dummy reversal. Usually, the declarer obtains extra trump tricks by ruffing his losers in dummy. In this case, South reverses that procedure by ruffing dummy's losers in his own hand. The result is that he gains the all-important twelfth trick.

First Things First

East dealer.
Both sides vulnerable.

```
                NORTH
              ♠ K Q J 8 4
              ♥ 3
              ♦ A Q 5 3
              ♣ 8 6 2
WEST                      EAST
♠ 7 6 3                   ♠ A 9 2
♥ Q 10 8 7 5 2            ♥ A J 4
♦ 9 6                     ♦ 7 2
♣ 5 4                     ♣ K J 10 9 3
                SOUTH
              ♠ 10 5
              ♥ K 9 6
              ♦ K J 10 8 4
              ♣ A Q 7
```

The bidding:

East	South	West	North
1 ♣	1 ♦	Pass	1 ♠
Pass	1 NT	Pass	3 ♦
Pass	3 NT		

Opening lead — seven of hearts.

You can reason out lots of things if you put your mind to it. You don't necessarily have to see the opponents' cards to know what they've got.

Look at this hand, for example, taken from a team match. At the first table, West led a heart and East made the smart play of the jack instead of the ace. If he had taken the ace and returned the jack, South would have ducked and then made four notrump by force.

But when East played the jack, South was afraid West had the ace and that the entire heart suit would be run against

him. He therefore won with the king. This didn't work out well, because East promptly took the ten of spades at trick two and played the ace and another heart. The result was that South went down two.

At the second table, the same contract was reached, and here also West led a heart and East played the jack.

But the declarer at this table analyzed the situation more carefully and made four notrump. He saw he would surely lose the contract if he took the jack with the king. He realized that the best he could do was cash eight tricks if he won the opening lead.

He could not be certain East had the ace of hearts, though it was very likely in the light of his opening bid, but he did not concern himself much with this problem.

What this declarer realized was that the contract was sure to be defeated if he won the first trick. He knew he couldn't make the hand unless East had the ace of hearts, and he therefore assumed that East had that card.

This was simply in line with the general theory that if a contract can be made only if the adverse cards are divided in a certain way, the declarer must proceed on the basis that that division exists. The danger of going down an extra trick is a negligible factor.

Giving
Declarer
Rope

North dealer.
North-South vulnerable.

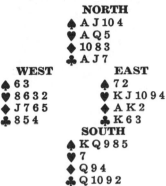

NORTH
♠ A J 10 4
♥ A Q 5
♦ 10 8 3
♣ A J 7

WEST
♠ 6 3
♥ 8 6 3 2
♦ J 7 6 5
♣ 8 5 4

EAST
♠ 7 2
♥ K J 10 9 4
♦ A K 2
♣ K 6 3

SOUTH
♠ K Q 9 8 5
♥ 7
♦ Q 9 4
♣ Q 10 9 2

The bidding:

North	East	South	West
1 NT	2 ♥	3 ♠	Pass
4 ♠			

Opening lead—two of hearts.

A basic rule of defense is that you try in every way possible to beat the contract. This may be impossible in some hands, because declarer just has too much ammunition, but most of the time the battle is close and the outcome depends on how well each side handles its cards.

Always the defense keeps its eye on the goal. For example, in this hand, the aim of the defense is to win four tricks. Imagine you're sitting East and defending against four spades.

West leads the two of hearts and dummy wins with the ace. Right away you make a mental note that your partner led his fourth best heart, which means, in turn, that declarer has a singleton. There are therefore no heart tricks possible for your side.

South takes two rounds of trumps and then leads the ten of clubs, which you win with the king. It is obvious your side cannot win any more tricks in spades, hearts or clubs, so your only hope lies in taking three diamond tricks.

This is not a difficult matter to arrange if your partner has the queen and declarer has as many as three diamonds. All you would have to do is cash two diamonds and continue the suit to let your partner take the setting trick.

However, you say to yourself that West may have the jack, not the queen. That possibility also offers a chance of defeating the contract, but you would destroy it if you first cashed the A-K.

The play that gives you the best chance of stopping the contract is to lead the two of diamonds. In the actual case, if you lead the deuce, South, who does not know you have the A-K, will most likely play low from his hand. If he does, he goes down. Thus, the low diamond return gives you the maximum chance of beating the hand.

Deep
Finesse

South dealer.
Neither side vulnerable.

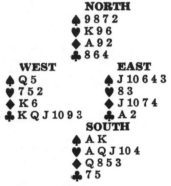

                    NORTH
                    ♠ 9 8 7 2
                    ♥ K 9 6
                    ♦ A 9 2
                    ♣ 8 6 4
    WEST   **EAST**
    ♠ Q 5   ♠ J 10 6 4 3
    ♥ 7 5 2   ♥ 8 3
    ♦ K 6   ♦ J 10 7 4
    ♣ K Q J 10 9 3   ♣ A 2
                    SOUTH
                    ♠ A K
                    ♥ A Q J 10 4
                    ♦ Q 8 5 3
                    ♣ 7 5

The bidding:

South	West	North	East
1 ♥	2 ♣	2 ♥	Pass
4 ♥			

Opening lead—king of clubs.

Good card reading is the most important single asset of the competent dummy player. Once declarer diagnoses the make-up of the opponents' hands, the battle is already half won.

There are two main sources that help declarer to determine how the defenders' cards are divided. One is the defenders' bidding, if any; the other is the knowledge he gains from the plays already made.

Take this case where, in effect, South played as though he had looked at the opponents' cards. At the critical point he made an unusual play that proved to be the key to the contract, but it was a play based on sound reasoning.

West led the king of clubs and East overtook it with the ace to return a club. West won with the nine and continued with the queen, East discarding a spade. Declarer ruffed, then drew three rounds of trumps, learning in the process that West had started with precisely three hearts and six clubs.

South now cashed the A-K of spades, everyone following suit, and led a low diamond. When West followed low, declarer played dummy's nine, which lost to the ten.

This unusual finesse paid off extremely well. East returned a spade and South ruffed. Declarer then played a low diamond to the ace, nailing West's king, and finessed the eight on the return, thus holding himself to only one diamond loser to make the contract.

This unusual method of handling the diamond combination became clearly marked once South had learned, from the play of the other suits, that West held no more than two diamonds. West was likely to hold the king of diamonds as part of his overcall, and it was therefore correct to play him for precisely K-x.

Exploring a Loophole

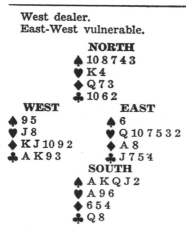

West dealer.
East-West vulnerable.

NORTH
- ♠ 10 8 7 4 3
- ♥ K 4
- ♦ Q 7 3
- ♣ 10 6 2

WEST
- ♠ 9 5
- ♥ J 8
- ♦ K J 10 9 2
- ♣ A K 9 3

EAST
- ♠ 6
- ♥ Q 10 7 5 3 2
- ♦ A 8
- ♣ J 7 5 4

SOUTH
- ♠ A K Q J 2
- ♥ A 9 6
- ♦ 6 5 4
- ♣ Q 8

The bidding:

West	North	East	South
1 ♦	Pass	1 ♥	1 ♠
Pass	Pass	2 ♥	2 ♠
3 ♥	3 ♠		

Opening lead—king of clubs.

Endplays take many different forms, but the general idea is that declarer puts one of the defenders on lead at a time when that defender will then be forced to lose a trick for his side regardless of what he returns.

Such endplay situations usually come about by design, since it is rare for the setting to occur naturally. The declarer plans his play so as to arrive at the winning position, but it sometimes happens that the defenders unwittingly help him to achieve the projected endplay.

Here is a case of this type. West led the king of clubs against the final contract of three spades and continued with the ace and another club.

Declarer ruffed, drew two rounds of trumps, and then proceeded to arrive at the position whereby he could cut his three natural diamond losers to two. This he did by cashing the king and ace of hearts, ruffing a heart in dummy, and then entering his hand with a trump.

When he now led a diamond, the defense could not function in any way that would bring them three diamond tricks. West did as well as he could by playing the nine, but declarer, keen to the situation, ducked in dummy.

It did not matter what East played on this trick. If he permitted the nine to hold, West would be unable to do better than return a diamond, whereupon East would win with the ace and be forced to give declarer a ruff and discard.

Similarly, if East overtook the nine with the ace and returned a diamond, dummy's queen would become a trick and that also would be the end of the road for the defense.

So South made three spades as the result of the endplay.

Of course, the contract could have been defeated if West had shifted to a diamond at either trick two or three. This would have permitted the defense to win two clubs and three diamonds to defeat the contract a trick.

Exotic Play

South dealer.
Neither side vulnerable.

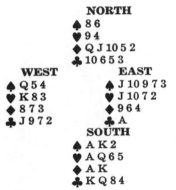

NORTH
♠ 8 6
♥ 9 4
♦ Q J 10 5 2
♣ 10 6 5 3

WEST
♠ Q 5 4
♥ K 8 3
♦ 8 7 3
♣ J 9 7 2

EAST
♠ J 10 9 7 3
♥ J 10 7 2
♦ 9 6 4
♣ A

SOUTH
♠ A K 2
♥ A Q 6 5
♦ A K
♣ K Q 8 4

The bidding:

South	West	North	East
3 NT	Pass	Pass	Pass

Opening lead—two of clubs.

There are plays in bridge that are sometimes described as fancy, yet cold analysis reveals that they are both logical and necessary.

Look at this hand, where South is in three notrump and West leads a club. Let's say East wins with the ace, dummy and declarer playing low, and returns the jack of spades.

South takes the ace, cashes the A-K of diamonds, and then plays the king of clubs, East showing out. This is the end of the road for South. He must now go down one or two tricks, depending upon how the subsequent play proceeds.

The outcome should not be surprising to declarer if he plays in this fashion, because the result is preordained. Dummy's good diamond tricks get lost in the shuffle because there is no entry to dummy to cash them. This lack of communication with dummy is obvious right away and the result can hardly be called unexpected.

But suppose South is a careful player who, when he sees this trouble coming up, takes steps to protect himself. Suppose, when East plays the ace of clubs on the first trick, South drops his queen on it.

This farsighted move eventually pays handsome dividends. South wins whatever card East returns at trick two, cashes the A-K of diamonds and the king of clubs, and then plays a low club towards dummy's ten.

This allows him to reach dummy either immediately or later and permits him ultimately to score ten tricks.

Dropping the queen of clubs on the ace might be called a fancy play, and perhaps it is, but it is surely a play that is called for by the particular circumstances. It practically guarantees the contract and is hence the right play, whether it be called fancy or not.

It is interesting to note that declarer does not even lose a trick by expending the queen on the ace. He still makes two club tricks, even though he wastes the queen. More important than that, he makes the contract.

Double-Barreled Action

South dealer.
Both sides vulnerable.

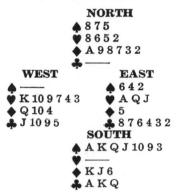

NORTH
♠ 8 7 5
♥ 8 6 5 2
♦ A 9 8 7 3 2
♣ ——

WEST
♠ ——
♥ K 10 9 7 4 3
♦ Q 10 4
♣ J 10 9 5

EAST
♠ 6 4 2
♥ A Q J
♦ 5
♣ 8 7 6 4 3 2

SOUTH
♠ A K Q J 10 9 3
♥ ——
♦ K J 6
♣ A K Q

The bidding:

South	West	North	East
2 ♠	Pass	3 ♦	Pass
7 ♠			

Opening lead—jack of clubs.

A reader sends this hand in which he bid and made seven spades. North-South were using the ace-showing convention over two-bids, and South wasted no time getting to seven after he learned that North had the ace of diamonds.

It is not easy to see how declarer made the contract, and if you feel like testing your skill before reading on, this is your chance.

Declarer ruffs the club in dummy, trumps a heart, and then ruffs a club, ruffs a heart, ruffs a club, and ruffs the third round of hearts.

He next draws three rounds of trumps, and, nine tricks hav-ing been played, this becomes the position:

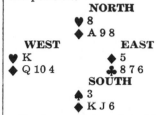

NORTH
♥ 8
♦ A 9 8

WEST
♥ K
♦ Q 10 4

EAST
♦ 5
♣ 8 7 6

SOUTH
♠ 3
♦ K J 6

Declarer now cashes his last trump. West cannot find a suitable discard. He is squeezed.

If West discards the king of hearts, dummy's eight becomes a trick, and if West chooses instead to discard a diamond, declarer's diamonds all become good. Either way, South wins the remaining tricks.

At first blush, it does seem overly-dramatic for South to trump the A-K-Q of clubs in dummy, but if he doesn't do this, he goes down.

The purpose of these plays is to try to exhaust one defender of all his hearts and thus place the burden of guarding against the eight of hearts on the other defender.

Nothing can be lost by this effort, even though it may turn out to be a waste of time if the hearts are divided 5-4.

If that proves to be the case, declarer can always fall back on a favorable diamond division, and will not be worse off for having given himself an extra choice to make the contract. Two shots to make the hand are better than one.

A Comedy of Errors

South dealer.
Both sides vulnerable.

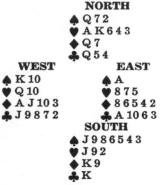

```
                    NORTH
                    ♠ Q 7 2
                    ♥ A K 6 4 3
                    ♦ Q 7
                    ♣ Q 5 4
        WEST                    EAST
        ♠ K 10                  ♠ A
        ♥ Q 10                  ♥ 8 7 5
        ♦ A J 10 3              ♦ 8 6 5 4 2
        ♣ J 9 8 7 2            ♣ A 10 6 3
                    SOUTH
                    ♠ J 9 8 6 5 4 3
                    ♥ J 9 2
                    ♦ K 9
                    ♣ K
```

The bidding:

South	West	North	East
Pass	Pass	1♥	Pass
1♠	Pass	Pass	Pass

Opening lead—nine of clubs.

World championships are tense affairs where the players go all out and do everything they can to record their feats for the benefit of posterity. The light moments are few, but here is one enacted in Budapest way back in 1937. The names of the contestants are mercifully omitted.

The contract was one spade. North decided there was no game in the hand after his partner had passed originally and merely responded with a spade to the opening heart bid. He therefore passed one spade. North's judgment was in a sense correct, because it turned out that the enemy could take the A-K of spades and two side aces to hold the contract to three spades.

However, the defense didn't function well and South did better than that. West led the nine of clubs. Declarer played low from dummy and so did East. South won with the king and led the nine of diamonds, winning in dummy with the queen.

He then played a low club. East was afraid that his partner had led originally from the 9-8-7-2 of clubs, which would give South the K-J alone, so he went up with the ace to prevent the jack from winning.

Declarer ruffed, of course, and entered dummy with a heart to discard his king of diamonds on the queen of clubs. Still not completely satisfied with having stolen two tricks, South decided to try and purloin one more.

He ruffed a diamond and led a low spade toward the queen. West was determined not to let the king of spades also be stolen from him, so he went up with the king.

The king held the trick for a moment—until East won it with the ace. When the queen of hearts fortunately dropped later, South was able to state with pride that he had made twelve tricks on the hand. His one regret was that he had been unable to find a way of shutting out the ace of trump!

A Good Offense
Is the Best Defense

North dealer.
Both sides vulnerable.

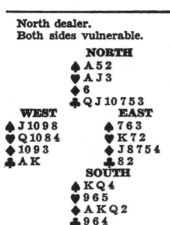

NORTH
♠ A 5 2
♥ A J 3
♦ 6
♣ Q J 10 7 5 3

WEST
♠ J 10 9 8
♥ Q 10 8 4
♦ 10 9 3
♣ A K

EAST
♠ 7 6 3
♥ K 7 2
♦ J 8 7 5 4
♣ 8 2

SOUTH
♠ K Q 4
♥ 9 6 5
♦ A K Q 2
♣ 9 6 4

The bidding:

North	East	South	West
1 ♣	Pass	1 ♦	Pass
2 ♣	Pass	2 NT	Pass
3 NT			

Opening lead—jack of spades.

Put yourself in the West seat for a moment and imagine that all you see is dummy's hand and your own. You lead the jack of spades originally and South wins it with the king, East playing the three. You take the club return with the king and it's now your play. What would you do at this point?

Actually, there's only one proper card to play now—the ten of hearts. If you lead it, declarer goes down; if you lead anything else, South makes the contract.

If declarer takes the ten with the ace, you wind up with three heart tricks and two clubs. If

declarer covers the ten with the jack, East wins with the king and returns the seven to establish your hearts, while if declarer ducks the ten, so does your partner. A heart continuation then establishes the heart tricks you need.

Note that if you lead a low heart at trick three instead of the ten, declarer ducks in dummy and then cannot be prevented from making four notrump.

Now how are you supposed to know to lead the ten of hearts? Well, let's look at it this way. You can count eight tricks for the declarer — three spades, a heart and four clubs—if you stand pat by making a "safe" lead of another spade. Obviously this can get you nowhere, because South is bound to be able to take at least one more trick from his hand on the bidding he put up.

No, you've got to attack to succeed. There are only two suits where South can be vulnerable—hearts or diamonds. Of the two, by far the more likely one is hearts. For a diamond shift to be right would require partner to have something like the A-Q-J of the suit, and that is hardly likely.

But for East to have the king of hearts is by no means a remote possibility. That's why you attack in hearts, being careful, of course, to lead the ten to protect against South's having the nine.

An Educated Guess

North dealer.
North-South vulnerable.

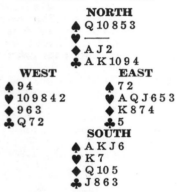

NORTH
♠ Q 10 8 5 3
♥ —
♦ A J 2
♣ A K 10 9 4

WEST
♠ 9 4
♥ 10 9 8 4 2
♦ 9 6 3
♣ Q 7 2

EAST
♠ 7 2
♥ A Q J 6 5 3
♦ K 8 7 4
♣ 5

SOUTH
♠ A K J 6
♥ K 7
♦ Q 10 5
♣ J 8 6 3

The bidding:

North	East	South	West
1 ♣	1 ♥	1 ♠	Pass
2 ♥	Pass	2 NT	Pass
4 ♠	Pass	6 ♠	

Opening lead—ten of hearts.

Lots of so-called guesses in the play of the cards are not actually guesses when you examine them closely. For example, take this deal where the contract is six spades and West leads a heart.

It is clear that South will go down one if, after ruffing the heart and drawing trumps, he follows the normal procedure of cashing the A-K of clubs in the hope of dropping the queen. Declarer would lose not only a club, but also a diamond when he later attempted a finesse in that suit.

Misguessing the club can be marked up to bad luck, if you're so minded, but actually, South can practically assure the contract by following a different line of play.

After ruffing the heart lead in dummy, he enters his hand with a trump and ruffs the king of hearts. He then cashes the ace of clubs and plays another trump to his hand.

Once declarer learns the spades are divided 2-2, the contract is certain to make. He leads a second club at this point. If West shows out, as might happen, dummy wins with the king and puts East on lead with a club. East has to return a diamond or a heart, either of which gives South the rest of the tricks.

If West follows to the club lead, declarer finesses the nine. If the finesse works, as it would in the actual case, twelve tricks become certain. Declarer loses at most a diamond trick.

If the finesse loses, meaning East was dealt the Q-x of clubs, the contract is likewise certain to make. East wins the queen, but has no safe card to return. A heart return permits South to discard a diamond and put his other diamond loser on dummy's fifth club, while a diamond return from East proves equally ineffective.

The so-called guess in clubs is not really a guess at all, so far as making the contract is concerned. South takes steps to assure the hand without worrying whether or not he guesses the true club situation.

For Whom
the Bell
Tolls

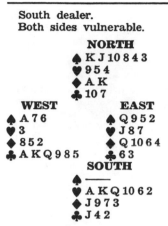

South dealer.
Both sides vulnerable.

NORTH
♠ K J 10 8 4 3
♥ 9 5 4
♦ A K
♣ 10 7

WEST
♠ A 7 6
♥ 3
♦ 8 5 2
♣ A K Q 9 8 5

EAST
♠ Q 9 5 2
♥ J 8 7
♦ Q 10 6 4
♣ 6 3

SOUTH
♠ —
♥ A K Q 10 6 2
♦ J 9 7 3
♣ J 4 2

The bidding:

South	West	North	East
1♥	2♣	2♠	Pass
3♥	Pass	4♥	

Opening lead—king of clubs.

Now wouldn't it be wonderful if every time you were declarer and had an opportunity to make an exceptionally smart play, someone would ring a bell to warn you that this was the moment to slow down and put on your thinking cap?

The trouble with these plays you hear about is that they sneak up on you unawares, and your opportunity to make them flits by before you even know it. But if only somebody'd ring a bell!

Here's one, for example, that would be easy to miss if you weren't watching for it. West leads the king of clubs and continues with the ace, East playing high-low. West then plays the queen of clubs which you ruff with the nine, East over-ruffing with the jack.

East returns a trump and there you are with all the rest of the tricks except for two diamonds that have to be taken care of. You can ruff one of them in dummy but not the other, because dummy has only one trump left.

You might get lucky and make the hand if the queen of diamonds dropped in the course of leading three rounds of the suit, but when you try it, the queen doesn't fall and down you go.

Well, what's wrong with the picture, you ask? The answer is that if you played the hand this way you goofed. You shoulda made the hand, that's what. The fact is that when East played high-low in clubs and asked his partner to continue the suit, he pretty well marked himself as able to over-ruff dummy with the jack.

So, on the third round of clubs, instead of ruffing, you should have discarded a spade from dummy. From then on, they wouldn't have been able to beat you with a crowbar.

A trump return would do the opposition no good, and neither would any other line of defense chosen by them.

Somebody shoulda rung a bell at trick three!

Lopping
Off
a Loser

West dealer.
Both sides vulnerable.

```
                    NORTH
                    ♠ Q 7
                    ♥ A 8 3
                    ♦ 9 6 5 2
                    ♣ 10 6 4 2
        WEST                    EAST
        ♠ —                     ♠ J 10 9 4
        ♥ K J 7 6 2             ♥ 10 5
        ♦ K Q 10 4             ♦ J 8 7 3
        ♣ K J 8 3             ♣ Q 9 7
                    SOUTH
                    ♠ A K 8 6 5 3 2
                    ♥ Q 9 4
                    ♦ A
                    ♣ A 5
```

The bidding:

West	North	East	South
1 ♥	Pass	Pass	2 ♠
Pass	3 ♠	Pass	4 ♠

Opening lead—king of diamonds.

You don't ever take things for granted if you're a really careful declarer. Instead, you assume the worst may happen and then make every possible effort to guard against it.

Here's a hand where it would be easy to go wrong, and yet, if you think the matter over, there's no good reason for falling down on the job.

Suppose you're South, playing four spades, and West leads the king of diamonds. There seems to be nothing to the hand when dummy comes down—you have two hearts and a club to lose—and everything looks fine.

But yet, being careful, you say to yourself it's possible to

go down; after all, trumps have been known to break 4-0. So this starts you thinking that maybe something can be done to cover this possibility.

There's one quick way of finding out whether trumps are going to break all right, and that's by leading them. So you play the ace of spades, on which West shows out, and your worst fears are realized.

Now a challenging problem has arisen. You have to lose a club and a spade, come what may, and the only way to salvage the hand is to cut your heart losers from two to one. This presents a special question —how the opponents' hearts can be divided so that only one heart trick will be lost.

A little thought brings the answer. West overcalled with two hearts, but he doesn't necessarily have to have the K-J-10 for his bid. East may have one of the honors, despite his pass. If this is the case, a satisfactory solution is possible.

Accordingly, you lead a spade to the queen and return a low heart from dummy. When East follows low, you play the nine. West takes the jack and returns a diamond which you ruff.

You cash the king of spades and then lead the queen of hearts, hoping for the best. It doesn't matter whether or not West covers. The king and ten are trapped and you lose only one heart trick, thus making the contract.

An Unusual Auction

West dealer.
North-South vulnerable.

NORTH
♠ 10 9
♥ A K J 9 7 6 2
♦ A 4
♣ J 3

WEST
♠ K Q J 8 7
6 4 2
♥ 4
♦ K J 5
♣ 6

EAST
♠ 3
♥ 8 5 3
♦ Q 10 8 7 6 2
♣ 9 7 5

SOUTH
♠ A 5
♥ Q 10
♦ 9 3
♣ A K Q 10 8 4 2

The bidding:

West	North	East	South
1 ♠	2 ♥	Pass	3 NT
4 ♠	4 NT	Pass	Pass
5 ♠	Pass	Pass	6 ♣
6 ♠	Pass	Pass	Dble
Pass	6 NT	Pass	Pass
7 ♠	Pass	Pass	7 NT
Dble			

Opening lead—king of spades.

My son Mike reports this hand played in a pair tournament. He was North and overcalled the spade bid with two hearts. He had no idea at this point that his side would wind up at seven notrump after a very unusual sequence of bids.

South had a wide choice of bids over two hearts. He knew there was a game somewhere, but couldn't be exactly sure of where it was. A slam didn't seem likely, in view of West's opening bid, but a game was highly probable.

He could have made a cuebid in spades in an effort to find the best spot, and he could also have jumped directly to four hearts. But South decided, playing match point duplicate, that the best score might lie in notrump. So he jumped to three notrump, deliberately courting the danger that a diamond suit would be run against him.

West, not vulnerable, bid four spades, and North bid four notrump. This had nothing to do with Blackwood, but was merely a raise in notrump.

West then bid five spades, which North passed. The pass indicated a willingness to have partner go on; otherwise, North would have doubled. South accepted the challenge, mentioning clubs for the first time.

West now bid six spades, which South doubled after two passes, but North, unwilling to accept a small penalty in lieu of a probable slam, converted to six notrump.

When East passed, West realized the slam would surely be made, so he "sacrificed" with seven spades. This didn't turn out well, because North passed again, once more inviting partner to continue with an appropriate hand.

South read the pass correctly and contracted for seven notrump. West had now run out of spade bids, so he doubled.

South had no trouble making seven, but the manner in which the grand slam in notrump was reached is certainly one of the strangest I have ever heard of.

Two Chances
Are Better
Than One

North dealer.
North-South vulnerable.

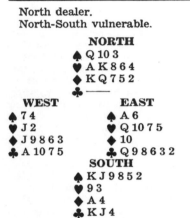

NORTH
♠ Q 10 3
♥ A K 8 6 4
♦ K Q 7 5 2
♣ —

WEST
♠ 7 4
♥ J 2
♦ J 9 8 6 3
♣ A 10 7 5

EAST
♠ A 6
♥ Q 10 7 5
♦ 10
♣ Q 9 8 6 3 2

SOUTH
♠ K J 9 8 5 2
♥ 9 3
♦ A 4
♣ K J 4

The bidding:

North	East	South	West
1 ♥	Pass	1 ♠	Pass
2 ♦	Pass	3 ♠	Pass
5 ♠	Pass	6 ♠	

Opening lead — seven of spades.

Suppose you were declarer at six spades and West led a trump and East took the ace and returned a trump. How would you play the hand?

There doesn't seem to be much to the play, but yet the hand is worthy of serious thought. To begin with, if you can make the slam but wind up going down one, you score minus 100 instead of plus 1,630 points. That makes a difference of 1,730 points, and that ain't hay in any language.

Suppose, after you win the trump return, you cashed the A-K of diamonds, which is one of the ways to play the hand. In the actual deal, East would show out on the second diamond lead and you would then find the slam difficult to make. You would have a legitimate squawk coming because it is unlucky to find the adverse diamonds divided 5-1, but we doubt that this would enlist a great deal of sympathy from the opponents.

Analysis would reveal that if you had commenced by first cashing the A-K of hearts and ruffing a heart, the hand would be made. You could then trump a club in dummy, ruff another heart, and claim the balance. The K-J of clubs would be discarded on the fifth heart in dummy and a high diamond.

That is really the right way to play the hand. By attacking hearts first, you assure the contract if the suit is divided 3-3 or 4-2, regardless of how the diamonds are divided. If it turns out that the hearts are (unluckily) divided 5-1, you can still switch over to diamonds and make the contract if that suit is divided 3-3 or 4-2.

But if you commence by playing diamonds first and get a bad break, you will pretty surely be sunk unless the hearts are specifically divided 3-3.

By playing hearts first, you are sure to make the slam if *either* suit is divided 3-3 or 4-2. Attacking hearts first is therefore the indicated play.

Pursuing
the
Impossible

East dealer.
East-West vulnerable.

                    NORTH
                    ♠ K J
                    ♥ 7 4 3
                    ♦ A J 10 8 4
                    ♣ A 9 7
WEST   **EAST**
♠ 6 3   ♠ Q 10 4
♥ 6   ♥ A Q J 10 8
♦ 9 7 6   ♦ 5 2
♣ Q J 10 8 5   ♦ 5 2
3 2   ♣ K
                    SOUTH
                    ♠ A 9 8 7 5 2
                    ♥ K 9
                    ♦ K Q 3
                    ♣ 6 4

The bidding:

East	South	West	North
1♥	1♠	Pass	2♦
Pass	3♦	Pass	3♠
Pass	4♠		

Opening lead—six of hearts.

There is no use trying to perform the impossible in bridge, which is what South attempted to do in this hand.

The bidding was certainly reasonable. South overcalled with a spade and then raised two diamonds to three. North showed his spade support by bidding three spades, and South naturally went to four.

West led a heart. East took the ace and returned a heart which West ruffed. West then played a club.

Declarer won with the ace, cashed the king of spades, and led the jack, East covering with the queen and West showing out.

South had lost two heart tricks and now also had a trump trick to lose. In an effort to escape the club loser, he cashed the K-Q of diamonds and played a diamond to the ten, hoping East would follow suit, in which case he would be able to discard a club on the next diamond lead.

But East ruffed and South eventually had to concede a club trick to go down one.

Obviously, South failed to realize that this method of play was sure to fail. If he had thought the matter over, he would have known he was attempting the impossible.

East had shown up with a seven-card heart suit — conclusively proved when West ruffed a heart at trick two. East was also known to have started with three spades — neither more nor less. Furthermore, East had followed suit (with the king) when West returned a club at trick three.

Eleven of East's cards in three suits were thus accounted for early in the play, and it therefore became impossible for East to have more than two cards in the fourth. suit, diamonds.

South should therefore have led a spade at trick six and given East his trump trick then and there. If he had done this, he would have made the contract. He should have played for what was possible — that East had a singleton club; not for what was impossible — that East had three diamonds.

A Generality
Is Only
a Generality

East dealer.
Both sides vulnerable.

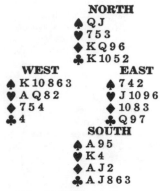

NORTH
♠ Q J
♥ 7 5 3
♦ K Q 9 6
♣ K 10 5 2

WEST
♠ K 10 8 6 3
♥ A Q 8 2
♦ 7 5 4
♣ 4

EAST
♠ 7 4 2
♥ J 10 9 6
♦ 10 8 3
♣ Q 9 7

SOUTH
♠ A 9 5
♥ K 4
♦ A J 2
♣ A J 8 6 3

The bidding:

East	South	West	North
Pass	1 NT	Pass	3 NT

Opening lead—six of spades.

It is perfectly normal for anyone who reads books on bridge to follow the advice contained in those books.

Presumably, the author must be credited with knowing what he is talking about, and the principles he enunciates should be generally followed. However, the trouble is that the general principles set forth in these books are often taken too literally. The player should learn to govern the rule and not permit it to govern him.

For example, take the proposition that when you have nine cards of a suit and are missing the Q-x-x-x, it is better to cash the ace and king and hope to catch the queen than it is to finesse against the queen. This is a sound enough principle to follow in most hands, but the declarer should not close his eyes to the possibility of finessing when the circumstances call for it.

In this hand, for instance, where West leads a spade and dummy's jack wins, South should certainly not follow the general rule in dealing with the club suit.

At trick two he should cash the king of clubs and then play another club and finesse the jack when East follows low. South should not feel particularly concerned that the jack may lose to the queen, the reason being that even if that happens he can still point to ten sure tricks.

In the actual case, with the finesse working, South winds up with eleven tricks, but that is not the point at all. What is important is that by taking the club finesse he guarantees the contract whether or not the finesse is successful.

But let's say that South comes from the school that always plays the A-K when he has nine of a suit. Then, in the present case, he will go down if he continues with a club and East takes it into his head to shift to the jack of hearts.

South takes the club finesse as a protective measure. He can afford to lose a club trick to West, but not to East.

Don't
Give Up
the Ship

South dealer.
Both sides vulnerable.

```
                    NORTH
                    ♠ K 8 7 3
                    ♥ K 7 4
                    ♦ A 8 5
                    ♣ K J 2
     WEST                        EAST
     ♠ Q 10 2                    ♠ 5
     ♥ Q 6                       ♥ J 10 8 5 3
     ♦ Q 9 4 2                   ♦ J 7 6 3
     ♣ 9 8 7 3                   ♣ 10 6 4
                    SOUTH
                    ♠ A J 9 6 4
                    ♥ A 9 2
                    ♦ K 10
                    ♣ A Q 5
```

The bidding:

South	West	North	East
1 ♠	Pass	3 ♠	Pass
6 ♠			

Opening lead—nine of clubs.

No record is kept of the number of times that declarer concedes down one—even though there is a way of making the contract by playing on—but it must come to a sizable figure. Usually declarer throws in the sponge because he sees no possibility of avoiding defeat and simply can't wait to go on to the next deal, but this is not a healthy attitude to take and can cost many points.

Consider this deal where South was in a very reasonable six spade contract. He won West's club lead with the ace, played a spade to the king, and a spade back to the ace.

With East showing out on the second spade, South all too hastily conceded a trump and a heart for down one. The grateful opponents accepted the offer and chalked up 100 points for their side.

But declarer could have made the slam had he not become upset by the unfavorable trump break. He still had a legitimate chance for the contract after East showed out on the second trump, and he should have carried on in the hope that this chance would mature.

After taking the ace of spades at trick three, he should have attempted an elimination play to try to avoid the heart loser. In the actual case, this effort would have succeeded.

Declarer starts by cashing the K-A of diamonds and ruffing a diamond. He then cashes his remaining clubs and the A-K of hearts before putting West on lead with a trump.

At this point West has a diamond and a club left, while dummy and South each have a losing heart and a trump.

West, on lead, must yield a ruff and discard. Whatever he plays, South ruffs in one hand and discards a heart from the other, thus avoiding a heart loser and making the slam.

Never give up!

Bridge
Is an
Easy Game

South dealer.
Neither side vulnerable.

```
                    NORTH
                    ♠ A K 8 3
                    ♥ 9 5 3
                    ♦ K 6 4
                    ♣ K 9 2
        WEST                    EAST
        ♠ 9 4                   ♠ J 10 7 5 2
        ♥ Q J 10 8 4            ♥ 7 2
        ♦ Q J 3                 ♦ 10 9 8 5
        ♣ A J 8                 ♣ 10 7
                    SOUTH
                    ♠ Q 6
                    ♥ A K 6
                    ♦ A 7 2
                    ♣ Q 6 5 4 3
```

The bidding:

South	West	North	East
1 ♣	1 ♥	1 ♠	Pass
1 NT	Pass	3 NT	

Opening lead — queen of hearts.

Good technique is simply a matter of making the right play at the right time. This is not always easy to do, because many situations require precise and unfaltering reasoning, but most of the time the declarer has no trouble figuring out the proper play.

Take this hand where South plays three notrump after West overcalls in hearts. A heart is led and good technique requires declarer to let West win the trick. The purpose of ducking the queen is to interfere with subsequent communication between the East and West hands.

West continues with the jack and South takes the king. There is no hope of winning nine tricks without tackling clubs, so South plays a low club at trick three. West follows low, of course, and now South must play the nine to make the contract.

He doesn't expect the nine to win, and in fact it loses to the ten, but he plays the nine because he can afford to lose a club to East and another one later to West, but can't afford to lose both tricks to West.

The combination of ducking the heart on the first trick and playing the nine of clubs on the third trick makes the hand for South.

East wins the club, but, thanks to the opening play by South, East does not have a heart to return at this stage. Let's say he plays the ten of diamonds. South wins it and leads another club.

West can take his ace now or later, but that is the last trick for the defense. South winds up with ten tricks to make the contract.

Declarer's problem from the beginning is to prevent West from establishing and cashing his long heart suit. All his moves are directed to that end. The first step is to sever connections between East and West, and the second is to prevent West from winning two club tricks. Declarer just keeps his eye on the ball to make sure that both missions are accomplished.

Loser
on
Loser

South dealer.
Both sides vulnerable.

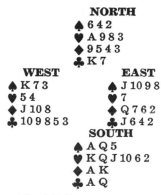

```
                    NORTH
                  ♠ 6 4 2
                  ♥ A 9 8 3
                  ♦ 9 5 4 3
                  ♣ K 7
    WEST                    EAST
  ♠ K 7 3                 ♠ J 10 9 8
  ♥ 5 4                   ♥ 7
  ♦ J 10 8                ♦ Q 7 6 2
  ♣ 10 9 8 5 3            ♣ J 6 4 2
                   SOUTH
                 ♠ A Q 5
                 ♥ K Q J 10 6 2
                 ♦ A K
                 ♣ A Q
```

The bidding:

South	West	North	East
2 ♥	Pass	3 ♥	Pass
4 NT	Pass	5 ♦	Pass
5 NT	Pass	6 ♦	Pass
6 ♥			

Opening lead—ten of clubs.

Suppose you're playing a contract the result of which appears to depend upon the success of a particular finesse. It is then your duty to look a little further into the matter to see whether or not there is a way of increasing your chances beyond the 50% probability of winning the finesse.

This principle, and what stems from it, is a powerful weapon in the arsenal of any good player. The mere thought of a finesse should stir up a chain reaction that starts a search for a way of avoiding the finesse.

For example, look at this hand where South is in six hearts. On the surface, it seems that declarer will have to rely on a successful spade finesse to make the contract. However, there is a decided possibility of making the slam even though West has the king of spades, and it costs declarer nothing to investigate this possibility before attempting the finesse.

Accordingly, he wins the club lead with the ace and cashes the K-Q of hearts and A-K of diamonds. He notes that West plays the 10-8 of diamonds as that suit is led. Declarer next enters dummy with the king of clubs and plays the five of diamonds.

East cannot afford to step up with the queen because that would catch West's jack and promote the nine into a trick, so he plays low on the diamond.

South does not ruff the diamond because there is a strong possibility that West started with only the J-10-8 or Q-10-8 of diamonds. He discards a spade loser instead. West is forced to win the trick with the jack and cannot make a play that does not give declarer the rest of the tricks.

This line of play succeeds because the diamonds are favorably divided, but note that if the diamond situation were unfavorable, South would still have the spade finesse to fall back on. The whole point is that South greatly increases his chances of making the slam by first sounding out the diamond suit.

It Takes
Two
to Tango

North dealer.
Both sides vulnerable.

```
              NORTH
              ♠ A Q 9 4
              ♥ 4
              ♦ 7 6 2
              ♣ A Q J 8 3
  WEST                    EAST
♠ 6 3                    ♠ 10 8 7 5 2
♥ K J 8 5 2              ♥ A 6 3
♦ K 10 4                 ♦ J 9 5
♣ 7 5 4                  ♣ K 6
              SOUTH
              ♠ K J
              ♥ Q 10 9 7
              ♦ A Q 8 3
              ♣ 10 9 2
```

The bidding:

North	East	South	West
1 ♣	Pass	1 ♦	Pass
1 ♠	Pass	2 NT	Pass
3 NT			

Opening lead—five of hearts.

Good defense depends largely on partnership cooperation. The defenders always try to help each other in pursuing their mutual goal of trying to overcome the declarer. In uniting their efforts to accomplish this, they lean heavily on universally accepted defensive conventions.

Examine the play of this hand, which shows how important it is for the defensive side to send messages to one another with accuracy. West opens the five of hearts, the fourth best card of his longest suit. East wins with the ace and returns the six on which South plays the nine.

If West makes the mistake of winning the nine with the jack, South makes the contract. There is no hope for the defense after this. Whatever West returns, declarer establishes his clubs to guarantee nine tricks.

But if West plays the two of hearts on the nine (thus disclosing he started with five hearts), South is defeated regardless of which way he turns. His best play, a club finesse, loses to the king, and back comes a heart to sink the ship.

Now how is it that West is smart enough to duck the nine of hearts at trick two? Must not his nerves be made of iron to resist the impulse to win the trick? No, not at all. Ducking is simply the right play to make and that is why he makes it.

He knows from the return of the six that that is the highest heart East has left. This means that South started with the Q-10-9-7 and that there is no chance of running the suit immediately. By ducking the nine, he relies on the hope that East has a solid entry in clubs or spades so that another, more deadly, heart lead can be made by East.

West realizes, of course, that East may have neither of the black kings, but he knows that if this is the case there is no hope for the defense. He therefore adopts the only line of defense that can possibly succeed.

The Uppercut

West dealer.
East-West vulnerable.

```
                NORTH
                ♠ K 8 3
                ♥ 7
                ♦ 10 9 4 2
                ♣ A K Q 10 5
    WEST                    EAST
    ♠ J 10 5               ♠ Q 7 4 2
    ♥ A 6 4                ♥ 9 8 5
    ♦ A K Q 7 6            ♦ 5 3
    ♣ 8 3                  ♣ 9 7 6 2
                SOUTH
                ♠ A 9 6
                ♥ K Q J 10 3 2
                ♦ J 8
                ♣ J 4
```

The bidding:

West	North	East	South
1 ♦	2 ♣	Pass	4 ♥

Opening lead—king of diamonds.

The uppercut is a colorful term used to describe the promotion of defensive trump tricks in suit contracts. By any other name the play would be equally effective, but in all pertinent cases it leaves the declarer with a feeling that someone has pulled the rug from under his feet.

Superficially, it would seem that South must make four hearts, losing two diamonds and a heart, but actually, South has to go down one against the best defense.

West leads the K-Q of diamonds and then follows with a low diamond which East trumps with the eight. Declarer is forced to overruff—otherwise he goes down immediately—so let's say he trumps with the ten and leads the jack of hearts.

This presents a problem of sorts to West, who might think his partner could win the jack if he ducked, but West takes the trick with the ace because he realizes that South would not have jumped to four hearts except with excellent trumps, as well as the ace of spades.

From West's viewpoint, the best chance of beating the contract is to play East to have the nine of hearts. So, after taking the ace of hearts, he leads another low diamond, hoping for another well-directed uppercut from East.

East does not let him down in this hand because, when he ruffs with the nine, it forces the queen from South, and that leaves declarer with the K-3-2 of trumps, while West still has the 6-4 left. As a result, West must make another heart trick, and South's apparently solid trumps turn out to be an optical illusion.

Note that West's defensive campaign, while it takes a little time to mature, is a practical one. He has a far greater chance, on the bidding, of finding East with several intermediate sized trumps than he does of finding East with a high-card trick.

Accordingly, West plays for the double-uppercut from the start, aiming to establish his lowly six as the setting trick.

The Night Before Christmas

'Twas the night before Christmas,
  Two guests in our house
Had started to play bridge
  With me and my spouse.

"Please tell me," she shouted,
  "Why didn't you double?
'Twas plain from the start
  That we had them in trouble."

" 'Tis futile, my dear,"
  Said I, taking no stand,
"To discuss it with you—
  Let us play the next hand."

"Remember next time,"
  Said she, icing a frown,
"To double a contract
  That's sure to go down."

So I picked up my cards
  In a downtrodden state,
Then I opened One Spade
  And awaited my fate.

East dealer.
North-South vulnerable.

The guy sitting South
  Was like many I've known;
He played and he bid
  In a world all his own.

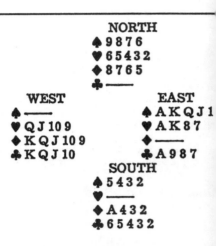

NORTH
♠ 9876
♥ 65432
♦ 8765
♣ —

WEST
♠ —
♥ QJ109
♦ KQJ109
♣ KQJ10

EAST
♠ AKQJ1
♥ AK87
♦ —
♣ A987

SOUTH
♠ 5432
♥ —
♦ A432
♣ 65432

"Two diamonds," he countered
  With scarcely a care;
The ace in his hand
  Gave him courage to spare.

My wife, she smiled faintly,
  And tossing her head,
Leaned over the table:
  "I double," she said.

And North, for some reason
  I cannot determine,
Bid Two Hearts as though
  He were preaching a sermon

I grinned as I doubled,
  Enjoying the fun,
And turned round to South
  To see where he would run.

But South, undistressed,
  Not at loss for a word,
Came forth with Two Spades—
  Did I hear what I heard?

The other two passed
  And in sheer disbelief
I said, "Double, my friend,
  That'll bring you to grief."

South passed with a nod,
  His composure serene;
My wife with a flourish
  Led out the heart queen.

I sat there and chuckled
  Inside o'er their fix—
But South very calmly
  Ran off eight straight tricks!

He ruffed the first heart
  In his hand right away,
And then trumped a club
  On the very next play.

He crossruffed the hand
  At a breathtaking pace
Till I was left holding
  Five spades to the ace.

In anguish my wife cried,
  "Your mind's growing old,
Don't you see six notrump
  In this hand is ice cold?"

By doubling this time
  I'd committed a sin.
It just goes to prove
  That you never can win.

Precision
Play

North dealer.
Both sides vulnerable.

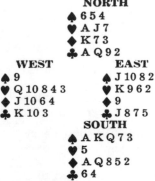

NORTH
♠ 6 5 4
♥ A J 7
♦ K 7 3
♣ A Q 9 2

WEST
♠ 9
♥ Q 10 8 4 3
♦ J 10 6 4
♣ K 10 3

EAST
♠ J 10 8 2
♥ K 9 6 2
♦ 9
♣ J 8 7 5

SOUTH
♠ A K Q 7 3
♥ 5
♦ A Q 8 5 2
♣ 6 4

The bidding:

North	East	South	West
1 ♣	Pass	1 ♠	Pass
1 NT	Pass	3 ♦	Pass
3 ♠	Pass	6 ♠	

Opening lead—four of hearts.

Dummy play is a logical process by which declarer can usually work out the best method of play.

Here is an example of the technique of dummy play. West leads a heart and South takes the ace and draws two rounds of trumps, discovering that East has a trump trick coming.

It is now clear that the contract cannot be made unless West has the king of clubs. Declarer therefore assumes at this point that the club finesse will work whenever it is attempted. To assume otherwise would be equivalent to conceding defeat.

Declarer also has to consider the diamond situation. He sees that if the diamonds are divided 3-2 he will make the contract, so he turns his thoughts to the possibility of a 4-1 division and what he can do to protect against that condition if it exists.

A little reflection convinces him that the 4-1 division can be overcome whether East has the four diamonds or West. Accordingly, he plays a diamond to the king and a diamond back.

As it happens, East has no more diamonds and discards a heart. (If East ruffs the diamond, South has an easy time making the rest of the tricks. If East had had the four diamonds, South would have cashed the A-Q and ruffed a diamond in dummy.)

So declarer wins with the queen of diamonds, finesses the queen of clubs, and plays another diamond. Once again East discards, since it would do him no good to ruff. South takes the ace of diamonds and next trumps a diamond in dummy.

It does not matter whether East overruffs or not. East can win a trump trick at this point or later, but, either way, South makes six spades as a result of careful play.

Note that declarer cannot make the hand if he does not play the diamonds in the indicated way. He must cash the king first and then twice lead diamonds from dummy towards his A-Q. To do otherwise would be fatal.

Elimination Play

South dealer.
Both sides vulnerable.

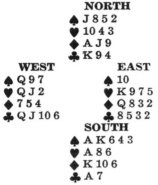

```
                    NORTH
                 ♠ J 8 5 2
                 ♥ 10 4 3
                 ♦ A J 9
                 ♣ K 9 4
      WEST                    EAST
   ♠ Q 9 7                  ♠ 10
   ♥ Q J 2                  ♥ K 9 7 5
   ♦ 7 5 4                  ♦ Q 8 3 2
   ♣ Q J 10 6               ♣ 8 5 3 2
                    SOUTH
                 ♠ A K 6 4 3
                 ♥ A 8 6
                 ♦ K 10 6
                 ♣ A 7
```

The bidding:

South	West	North	East
1 ♠	Pass	2 ♠	Pass
4 ♠			

Opening lead—queen of clubs.

The purpose of the elimination play is to save declarer a trick that he might otherwise lose. Declarer tries to set up a position which, when he thrusts one of the defenders into the lead, forces that player to make a lead favorable to the declarer.

South is in four spades and gets a club lead which he wins with the ace. He cashes the A-K of spades, hoping the queen will drop, but East shows out on the second spade and South then knows he must lose a trump trick.

Two heart losers are also certain. Since there are no club tricks to lose, the success of the hand depends upon whether or not declarer is able to escape a diamond loser.

This would be easy enough for South to arrange if he knew which defender had the queen of diamonds—he has a possible finesse against the queen in either direction—but since he doesn't know where the queen is located and doesn't want to guess, he falls back on the elimination play.

He cashes the king of clubs, ruffs a club, and then gives West his trump trick. By eliminating clubs from dummy, he forces West to return a heart. (West cannot afford a diamond or club return, either of which would be fatal.)

South wins the queen of hearts with the ace and exits with a heart. It does not matter whether West wins this heart trick and East the next one, or vice versa.

The defender who winds up on lead is then forced to play a diamond, thus relieving declarer of the necessity to guess the location of the queen of diamonds, or else to return a club or a heart, thus permitting declarer a ruff and discard. The elimination play is bound to succeed in all cases.

There are other variations by which South can attain the same favorable position, but the important thing is that South should rely upon the elimination play rather than his occult powers.

Silence
Is Golden

South dealer.
Neither side vulnerable.

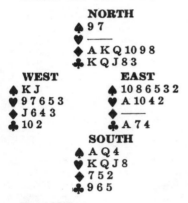

NORTH
♠ 9 7
♥ —
♦ A K Q 10 9 8
♣ K Q J 8 3

WEST
♠ K J
♥ 9 7 6 5 3
♦ J 6 4 3
♣ 10 2

EAST
♠ 10 8 6 5 3 2
♥ A 10 4 2
♦ —
♣ A 7 4

SOUTH
♠ A Q 4
♥ K Q J 8
♦ 7 5 2
♣ 9 6 5

The bidding:

South	West	North	East
1♣	Dble	6♣	Dble

Opening lead—king of spades.

It goes without saying that partners should not discuss a hand while it's in progress, and this applies especially to the defenders. However, we all know that in some games, the chatty ones, the rule is broken all the time.

The most famous hand where this rule was violated occurred, surprisingly enough, in a national championship.

The bidding was astonishing, to say the least. South probably should have passed, but he ventured a club. It would seem that, having paid his entrance fee, he wanted to get his money's worth. West was likewise a believer in the right of free speech, and he made an informatory (?) double.

North, who knew a good hand when he saw one, jumped to six clubs, which East, out of respect for his two aces, doubled.

West, on lead, struggled valiantly. Finally, in desperation, he opened the king of spades. Declarer won and played a club to the jack, losing to the ace. East returned a spade and South took it with the queen as East almost fell out of his chair.

East began to seethe inwardly as declarer led a club to the queen, West dropping the ten. But now East could contain himself no longer. He leaned forward, red-faced, and whispered so gently that he could be heard in the far reaches of the room: "You idiot! You could have led a heart, a diamond or a club and we'd have beaten the hand. But you, with your nimble brain, had to pick a spade."

South, who was neither blind, deaf, nor dumb, greeted this statement with cocked ear. He knew East was a fine analyst, and if a diamond could beat the slam, it meant that East had a void.

So declarer played a club to his nine, led a diamond, and finessed the eight. He had to, to make the slam.

The Theory of Fourth Best

North dealer.
East-West vulnerable.

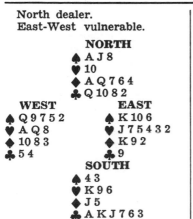

NORTH
♠ A J 8
♥ 10
♦ A Q 7 6 4
♣ Q 10 8 2

WEST
♠ Q 9 7 5 2
♥ A Q 8
♦ 10 8 3
♣ 5 4

EAST
♠ K 10 6
♥ J 7 5 4 3 2
♦ K 9 2
♣ 9

SOUTH
♠ 4 3
♥ K 9 6
♦ J 5
♣ A K J 7 6 3

The bidding:

North	East	South	West
1 ♦	Pass	2 ♣	Pass
3 ♣	Pass	5 ♣	

Opening lead—two of spades.

A reader asks whether I subscribe to the custom of leading the fourth best card on defense. Many players contend that such leads, by their very nature, help declarer more than the other defender.

It seems to me that defense is difficult enough without adding to it the guesswork and the uncertainties created by suppressing information valuable to partner or by introducing the deceptive factor. The key to good defense is good partnership rapport and seldom can a player succeed in fooling declarer without also fooling partner.

This deal illustrates the point. West led the two of spades—his fifth best spade—instead of the five, his fourth best. Dummy played the eight and East quite properly played the ten. When the ten held, East continued with the king.

Declarer took the ace, drew two rounds of trumps, led the jack of diamonds, and finessed. East won with the king and now had to find the right return to beat the contract.

He knew that West had the queen of spades because the ten had won the first trick. He also knew that West had led the deuce of spades, indicating a four-card suit. It followed from this that declarer had another spade to lose. So East returned a spade.

This proved fatal when declarer ruffed the spade and disposed of all his hearts on dummy's diamonds to bring home eleven tricks.

Now let's suppose that West had played normally and led his fourth best spade, the five. Again, East would have won with the ten and returned the king. Dummy would take the ace, but on this trick West would play the deuce to identify his five-card suit.

When East later took his king of diamonds, he would of course appreciate the futility of a spade return—since South could not have another spade—and he would return a heart to put declarer down one.

Making
Your
Luck

North dealer.
Neither side vulnerable.

NORTH
♠ K J 6
♥ A K Q
♦ A K J 4
♣ K J 3

WEST
♠ 10 9 8 7 5 3 2
♥ 9 6 4 2
♦ —
♣ 10 7

EAST
♠ A Q 4
♥ 10 7 5
♦ Q 10 6 8
♣ 8 5 2

SOUTH
♠ —
♥ J 8 3
♦ 9 8 7 5 2
♣ A Q 9 6 4

The bidding:

North	East	South	West
3 NT	Pass	4 ♦	Pass
5 ♦	Pass	6 ♦	

Opening lead—ten of spades.

The opening three notrump bid shows a balanced hand with 25 to 27 high-card points and strength in all suits. The bid is seldom used because you don't hold such hands often, but, when the occasion arises, the bid can be put to good use.

South didn't have much of a hand—only 7 points—but he had every reason to think he could make twelve tricks in one of his suits opposite a three notrump bid. So he bid four diamonds and went on to six after North had raised to five.

This contract would ordinarily have been easy to fulfill, but when he ruffed the spade lead and played a trump to the king, West showed out. Apparently East was destined to make two trump tricks, but South worked matters out so that East made only one of them.

In situations like this, declarer acts on the assumption that the rest of the cards are so divided that the hand can be made. The only hope of salvaging such contracts is to rely on an endplay to do East out of one of his tricks. In the present case, declarer starts by assuming that East's distribution is 4-3-3-3.

Accordingly, he ruffs a spade at trick three, enters dummy with a heart, and ruffs the last spade. Then he cashes three clubs and two more hearts.

By this time, since East has followed three times in each of the side suits, the outcome is a certainty. East has three cards left—the Q-10-6 of diamonds. Dummy has the A-J-4 of diamonds.

Whether declarer is in his own hand or in dummy at this point makes no difference. In either case he plays the four from dummy on the next trick.

East wins, but is then forced to lead a diamond into the A-J. It is true that South has to be lucky to find East with the right distribution after the disappointing 4-0 trump break, but that's the kind of luck all good players play for.

Now You See It Now You Don't

East dealer.
Neither side vulnerable.

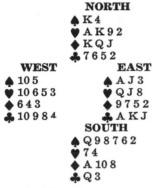

NORTH
♠ K 4
♥ A K 9 2
♦ K Q J
♣ 7 6 5 2

WEST
♠ 10 5
♥ 10 6 5 3
♦ 6 4 3
♣ 10 9 8 4

EAST
♠ A J 3
♥ Q J 8
♦ 9 7 5 2
♣ A K J

SOUTH
♠ Q 9 8 7 6 2
♥ 7 4
♦ A 10 8
♣ Q 3

The bidding:

East	South	West	North
1 NT	Pass	Pass	Dble.
Pass	Pass	2 ♣	Pass
Pass	3 ♠	Pass	4 ♠

Opening lead—ten of clubs.

Declarer had to play exceptionally well in this hand to make four spades. His apparent losers were two clubs and two spades, but he managed to make one trump loser disappear.

West led a club and East cashed the A-K and returned the jack. South ruffed and now had to find a way of losing only one spade trick.

Generally, with this suit combination, declarer begins by leading low towards the king. He hopes West was dealt A-x, and, if that is the case, the play succeeds. When West follows low, the king in dummy wins, and when the suit is returned, declarer simply plays low from his hand, forcing the ace. The queen later picks up East's remaining spade.

However, in this hand, South knew that the usual method of play could not succeed. Every missing high card was known to be in East's hand, since East had opened the bidding with a notrump (16 to 18 points). So he adopted a different line of play that gave him a chance of making the contract.

After ruffing the club, declarer cashed the A-K of hearts and trumped a heart. He then entered dummy with a diamond and ruffed the last club. He next cashed two diamonds, ending in dummy, at which point this was the situation:

North
♠ K 4
♥ 9

West
♠ 10 5
♥ 10

East
♠ A J 3

South
♠ Q 9 8

Declarer now led the nine of hearts. East realized that if he ruffed low, South would make the contract. So he ruffed with the jack, hoping to find West with the 10-9 or 10-8 of spades.

It was a good try by East, but South was not to be denied. He overruffed with the queen and led the eight of spades for a finesse. It didn't matter whether West covered or not. East could make only one trump trick.

About Percentage Plays

South dealer.
Neither side vulnerable.

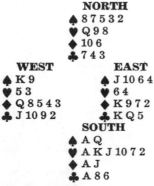

```
                NORTH
              ♠ 8 7 5 3 2
              ♥ Q 9 8
              ♦ 10 6
              ♣ 7 4 3
WEST                        EAST
♠ K 9                       ♠ J 10 6 4
♥ 5 3                       ♥ 6 4
♦ Q 8 5 4 3                 ♦ K 9 7 2
♣ J 10 9 2                  ♣ K Q 5
                SOUTH
              ♠ A Q
              ♥ A K J 10 7 2
              ♦ A J
              ♣ A 8 6
```

The bidding:

South	West	North	East
2 ♥	Pass	2 NT	Pass
3 ♥	Pass	4 ♥	

Opening lead—jack of clubs.

When declarer has a choice of ways to play a hand, he can do no better than follow the line of play that appears most likely to succeed.

Consciously or not, the skilled declarer follows this law of probabilities. He does not know how the defenders' cards are divided, but he bases his plays on what he considers to be the most probable division of their cards.

Here is a case where declarer failed to choose the best course of play and lost his contract as a result. He won the club lead with the ace, drew two rounds of trumps, ending in dummy, and finessed the queen of spades. This lost to the king, and he later lost two clubs and a diamond to go down one.

In effect, South gave himself about a 50% chance of making the contract by relying on East to have been dealt the king of spades. But he missed a different line of play which offered a far greater chance of success.

After winning the ace of clubs, he should have played the ace of spades and continued with the queen. Had he done this, he would have made the contract. West would take the king, and the defense would presumably cash two club tricks and return a diamond.

Declarer wins with the ace, plays a low heart to the eight, ruffs a low spade high, plays a low heart to the nine, and ruffs another spade high. By this time, dummy's fifth spade is established as a trick. South enters dummy with a trump and discards the jack of diamonds on the eight of spades.

This plan of play, for practical purposes, permits South to make the contract whenever the spades are divided 3-3 (36%) or 4-2 (48%).

The 84% probability of making the hand by relying on a favorable spade division is far more attractive than the 50% probability of East's having been dealt the king of spades. South treats the hand as though he had the A-x of spades instead of the A-Q.

76

A Fishy Deal

East dealer.
Both sides vulnerable.

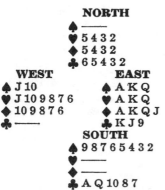

NORTH
♠ —
♥ 5 4 3 2
♦ 5 4 3 2
♣ 6 5 4 3 2

WEST
♠ J 10
♥ J 10 9 8 7 6
♦ 10 9 8 7 6
♣ —

EAST
♠ A K Q
♥ A K Q
♦ A K Q J
♣ K J 9

SOUTH
♠ 9 8 7 6 5 4 3 2
♥ —
♦ —
♣ A Q 10 8 7

Opening lead — ten of diamonds.

This is probably the most famous hand in the history of bridge. Legend has it that the Duke of Cumberland, some two centuries ago, held the East hand and backed it to the tune of 20,000 pounds against the North-South hands.

The Duke lost the wager as he was unable to score a trick despite his extraordinary array of high cards. Regardless of whether or not the tale is true or whether the hand was actually ever dealt, it comes to us from way back in the days of whist, having been first published by Edmond Hoyle in 1750.

No bidding is given with the Duke of Cumberland hand, the presumption being that some-how or other the final contract was seven clubs redoubled played by South.

There is no way of stopping the grand slam if declarer plays correctly. Aces become deuces as South destroys every honor card held by East.

Let's assume that West leads a diamond or a heart. Declarer ruffs, trumps a spade in dummy, and returns a club, capturing East's nine with the ten.

Declarer ruffs another spade in dummy, and again takes a trump finesse.

When declarer now ruffs the third round of spades in dummy, his remaining spades become established.

Declarer returns to his hand by ruffing either a diamond or a heart, cashes the ace of trumps, catching East's king, and chalks up all thirteen tricks as East's aces and kings fall like tenpins on South's good spades.

The deal is an extreme example of the destructive power of unusual distribution. Double and triple voids can very easily wreak havoc with point count and honor tricks.

Incidentally, we would like to respectfully suggest that if you ever play in a game with complete strangers and are dealt the East hand, you should either ask for a new deal or head quickly for the nearest exit!

One Peek
Is Worth
Two Finesses

West dealer.
Both sides vulnerable.

NORTH
♠ 9 7
♥ 7 5 4 2
♦ 8 7 6 5 3
♣ 10 3

WEST
♠ K
♥ Q 10 9 8 3
♦ A K Q 10
♣ 9 5 2

EAST
♠ 6 4 3 2
♥ K J
♦ 9 4
♣ Q J 8 7 6

SOUTH
♠ A Q J 10 8 5
♥ A 6
♦ J 2
♣ A K 4

The bidding:

West	North	East	South
1♥	Pass	1 NT	Dble
2♦	Pass	2♥	4♠

Opening lead—king of diamonds.

When I am asked what it takes to become a good bridge player, I usually say that the most important single faculty is the ability to reason well. Logic solves many difficult problems at the bridge table, and, in fact, sometimes works so well that the good player is unjustly suspected of using mirrors.

Look at this hand, for example, and follow the play. West led the A-K-Q of diamonds, declarer ruffing the third one. South then cashed the A-K of clubs and trumped a club, after which he led the nine of spades and went up with the ace, spearing the king and making the contract. He lost two diamonds and a heart.

Of course, anyone looking at all 52 cards would do just as well, seeing that West had the singleton king of spades, but the everyday player, not knowing the adverse cards, would finesse the spade and go down one.

This would be marked up to bad luck, no doubt, and that would be the end of the matter, but actually, the finesse is the wrong play and the ace is the right play.

Let's see why South should play the ace. First we go back to the bidding and see what can be learned there, and then we consider the plays on the first six tricks.

We're certain that West started with four diamonds and three clubs. We also know West must have either four or five hearts for his heart bid.

From that we can deduce that West started with one spade (if he has five hearts) or two spades (if he has four hearts). It therefore cannot do any good to finesse the spade, even if East has the king, because in that case East is bound to have been dealt K-x-x-x or K-x-x of spades.

Therefore, the only hope of avoiding a spade loser is that East has the x-x-x-x of spades. Since playing the ace offers some chance of making the contract, and finessing offers no chance of making the contract, the finesse is refused.

Follow the Odds

South dealer.
Neither side vulnerable.

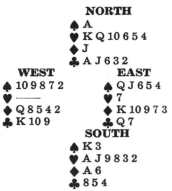

NORTH
♠ A
♥ K Q 10 6 5 4
♦ J
♣ A J 6 3 2

WEST
♠ 10 9 8 7 2
♥ ——
♦ Q 8 5 4 2
♣ K 10 9

EAST
♠ Q J 6 5 4
♥ 7
♦ K 10 9 7 3
♣ Q 7

SOUTH
♠ K 3
♥ A J 9 8 3 2
♦ A 6
♣ 8 5 4

The bidding:

South	West	North	East
1 ♥	Pass	3 ♣	Pass
3 ♥	Pass	6 ♥	

Opening lead—ten of spades.

The outcome of many hands played by declarer depends upon how he gauges the distribution of the opponents' cards. When he has no clues to guide him, either because the defenders did not bid at all or because their plays are not self-revealing, declarer cannot do better than depend on probabilities, that is, follow the line of play that would be most likely to succeed in the long run.

Examine this hand. South is in six hearts and West leads a spade. Every suit is under control except clubs. Here there is a danger of losing two tricks.

South knows that against certain combinations of cards held by East-West he can hold himself to one club loser if he plays correctly, and that against others he will have to lose two club tricks regardless of what he does.

South does not waste time devoting his thoughts to hands he cannot possibly make, but concentrates instead only on those where a favorable distribution of the cards will permit him to make the contract if he chooses the right line of play.

Accordingly, he wins the spade with the ace, plays a round of trump, cashes the king of spades and ace of diamonds, and ruffs a diamond in dummy. Then, after playing a heart to his hand, he leads a club, West producing the nine.

Now comes the crucial decision. If declarer plays the jack he is defeated because East wins and returns a club. But if he plays the ace he makes the contract. That is because, if East plays low on the ace, a club return forces East to yield a ruff and discard, while if East plays the queen on the ace, South can return to his hand with a trump and lead a club towards dummy.

The ace is the right play. For practical purposes, the jack play wins only when West has the K-Q. The ace play is successful whenever East has K-x-x, Q-x-x, K-x, Q-x, K or Q, and these possibilities outnumber those where West has the K-Q.

Substitution

South dealer.
Neither side vulnerable.

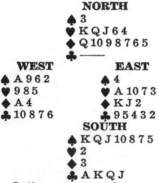

NORTH
- ♠ 3
- ♥ K Q J 6 4
- ♦ Q 10 9 8 7 6 5
- ♣ —

WEST
- ♠ A 9 6 2
- ♥ 9 8 5
- ♦ A 4
- ♣ 10 8 7 6

EAST
- ♠ 4
- ♥ A 10 7 3
- ♦ K J 2
- ♣ 9 5 4 3 2

SOUTH
- ♠ K Q J 10 8 7 5
- ♥ 2
- ♦ 3
- ♣ A K Q J

Let's say you become declarer at four spades with the South hand. West opens the ace of diamonds and continues with a diamond, which you ruff.

You then play the ten of spades which West ducks, and next the jack which West takes with the ace. He leads a heart to his partner's ace, and East then plays the king of diamonds.

It doesn't matter whether you ruff high or low—in either case, West is bound to make his nine of spades and down you go.

That's the story of the hand, if you played it that way, but naturally there's more to it than that. What we'd like to know is whether you can figure out a way to make the hand (you can), now that you know exactly how the East-West cards are divided.

Just as in most double-dummy problems, the solution isn't difficult once you've seen it. If you'd like to work out the answer for yourself, stop reading right here; otherwise, here it is:

The whole point is that you have to do something to prevent the defense from creating the overruff position in diamonds late in the play. Therefore, assuming that the first two leads are the ace and another diamond, you ruff the second one and play a club and trump it in dummy.

Now you lead the third round of diamonds, East playing the king, and on it you discard the two of hearts. That gives the defense its second trick, but the only other trick they can get after that is the ace of spades. East is out of diamonds and unable to make a return that will embarrass you in any way.

The purpose behind these plays was to remove a threatening card (the king of diamonds) from East's hand and at the same time discard a heart which had to be lost in any case.

It is not important that you wind up losing two diamond tricks instead of a heart and a diamond—what is important is that you lose only one trump trick instead of two.

Sylvia
Plays
Duplicate

North dealer.
Neither side vulnerable.

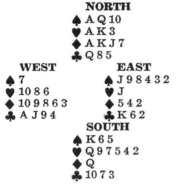

```
                NORTH
              ♠ A Q 10
              ♥ A K 3
              ♦ A K J 7
              ♣ Q 8 5
    WEST                  EAST
  ♠ 7                   ♠ J 9 8 4 3 2
  ♥ 10 8 6             ♥ J
  ♦ 10 9 8 6 3         ♦ 5 4 2
  ♣ A J 9 4            ♣ K 6 2
                SOUTH
              ♠ K 6 5
              ♥ Q 9 7 5 4 2
              ♦ Q
              ♣ 10 7 3
```

The bidding:

North	East	South	West
2 NT	Pass	3 ♥	Pass
4 ♥			

The night Sylvia played in her first duplicate at the club was a night to remember. She had been a member only three weeks (and had been playing bridge for scarcely more than that) when she was first exposed to the intricacies of tournament bridge.

Sylvia's exploits in the rubber bridge game at the club had already become a constant topic of conversation among the members, and no one dared predict the oddities that were certain to occur when she made her bow at duplicate.

Even allowing for her lack of experience, Sylvia's approach to the game was strikingly different from that of most beginners. Her thoughts ran in strange channels, and all her bids and plays—which to most people seemed unorthodox and even bizarre—were to her the very essence of natural play.

Of course, most of the time these innocent aberrations produced very poor results. However, Sylvia's penchant for the unusual occasionally did produce a fat dividend, and these spectacular successes would invariably keep the members buzzing like mad for weeks.

Take this deal from the duplicate. It was played at 13 tables, and at all of them the final contract was four hearts.

At nine tables West led a spade, at two tables West led a diamond, and at another table West led a trump. In each and every case declarer made 13 tricks.

It remained for Sylvia to conjure up a different lead. She wasn't trying to be brilliant — Sylvia always made the play that to her seemed proper—but she didn't know any better at the time. She led the jack of clubs!

This play had a devastating effect. East won dummy's queen with the king and returned a club. Sylvia cashed the A-9 and, not realizing that all the clubs were gone, returned the four. Declarer could do no better than discard from dummy, and East ruffed with the jack. South overruffed, but he now had to lose a trump trick to go down one!

The Long Distance View

South dealer.
Both sides vulnerable.

```
                NORTH
              ♠ A 10 5
              ♥ 6
              ♦ A 5 3
              ♣ A 10 9 7 4 2
    WEST                    EAST
  ♠ Q 6 3                 ♠ K 9 8 4
  ♥ Q J 10 7              ♥ K 8 4 3 2
  ♦ Q 10 6 2              ♦ J 9 7
  ♣ 8 5                   ♣ 6
                SOUTH
              ♠ J 7 2
              ♥ A 9 5
              ♦ K 8 4
              ♣ K Q J 3
```

The bidding:

South	West	North	East
1 ♣	Pass	3 ♣	Pass
3 NT	Pass	5 ♣	

Opening lead — queen of hearts.

There is no question that the majority of declarers have difclarers have difculty visualizing an end-play situation that will not arise until five or perhaps ten tricks after the opening lead is made.

However, the expert player quickly jumps the gap, seemingly without thought, accepting as routine the intermediate plays that lead to the end position.

For example, take this hand where the contract is five clubs and West leads a heart. South can see at once there are three possible losers—two spades and a diamond. He dismisses the thought of leading the spade suit himself because the odds are that he will lose two spade tricks if he does this.

Instead, he embarks on a line of play that will force the opponents to initiate the spade suit and thus assure the contract regardless of how the spades are divided. He starts the project by winning the ace of hearts and ruffing a heart in dummy.

He then enters his hand with a trump and ruffs his last heart in dummy. After drawing another round of trump (two, if necessary), he cashes the A-K of diamonds and exits with a diamond.

It does not matter to South which defender wins the trick or what suit is returned. He knows the contract is made regardless of how the opposing cards are divided.

Thus, in the actual case, if East took the third diamond lead, he would have to return a spade, thereby assuring South of only one spade loser, or else concede a ruff and discard.

And if West took the third diamond lead, he would run into the same dead end whether either defender had both the K-Q of spades, or whether the honors were divided. West, in such case, would be compelled to lead a spade honor (which dummy would win) or return a low spade (which dummy would duck).

By looking ahead and playing in this manner, South can be sure of the outcome from the word go.

Suspicion

North dealer.
Neither side vulnerable.

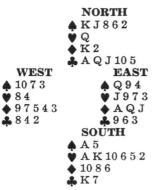

NORTH
♠ K J 8 6 2
♥ Q
♦ K 2
♣ A Q J 10 5

WEST
♠ 10 7 3
♥ 8 4
♦ 9 7 5 4 3
♣ 8 4 2

EAST
♠ Q 9 4
♥ J 9 7 3
♦ A Q J
♣ 9 6 3

SOUTH
♠ A 5
♥ A K 10 6 5 2
♦ 10 8 6
♣ K 7

The bidding:

North	East	South	West
1 ♣	Pass	1 ♥	Pass
1 ♠	Pass	3 ♥	Pass
3 ♠	Pass	4 ♥	

Opening lead — four of diamonds.

When a defender makes an unusual or unexpected play, declarer is obligated to ask himself why the play was made. He should not assume his opponents are trying to help him make the contract, but rather view any such play with at least mild suspicion. Today's hand illustrates the point.

West led a diamond and dummy's king lost to the ace. East cashed the queen and, in an effort to promote two trump tricks for himself, continued with the jack to force dummy to ruff.

Declarer ruffed, crossed to the ace of s p a d e s, and then cashed the A-K of hearts, leaving only the J-9 at large.

South could have continued with another heart at this point in the hope of f i n d i n g the trumps divided 1-1; had he done this he would quickly have gone down.

But declarer thought the matter over and decided that East had led the third round of diamonds in an effort to promote his trump holding. A f t e r all, East could have led a trump at trick three to prevent declarer from ruffing a diamond in dummy. Since he had led a diamond instead, South concluded that East had started originally with the J-9-x-x of hearts.

The problem now was to prevent East from winning two trump tricks with this holding. Only by executing a trump coup was this possible. Since South had to reduce his trump length to achieve the coup position, he led a s p a d e to the king and ruffed a spade to bring himself down to three trumps.

He next played a club to the ten and led the established jack of spades. East wisely discarded a club, but declarer, continuing his campaign, ruffed the spade to reduce his heart holding to the 10-6.

The king of clubs lead to the ace permitted South to play still another club from dummy, and East, with his J-9 in front of declarer's 10-6, could make only one trump trick.

Suit Preference in Notrump

North dealer.
Both sides vulnerable.

```
                NORTH
                ♠ 8
                ♥ Q J 10 5
                ♦ K J 4
                ♣ A Q J 8 7
    WEST                      EAST
    ♠ K 10 9 7 5 2            ♠ A 4 3
    ♥ A 3 2                   ♥ 8 7 4
    ♦ 9 8 6                   ♦ 7 5 2
    ♣ 4                       ♣ K 6 3 2
                SOUTH
                ♠ Q J 6
                ♥ K 9 6
                ♦ A Q 10 3
                ♣ 10 9 5
```

The bidding:

North	East	South	West
1 ♣	Pass	1 ♦	1 ♠
2 ♣	Pass	3 NT	

Opening lead — seven of spades.

Good defense requires good teamwork. It also requires a working knowledge of conventional signals. The defenders must help each other as much as possible during the play if they are to get the most out of their cards.

Look at this deal where the defense must function correctly if the contract is to be defeated. The hand occurred in a rubber bridge game.

South got to three notrump and West led a spade. East took the ace and returned the suit. West won and returned the ten to force out the queen.

Declarer led the ten of clubs and finessed, East playing low.

East was reluctant to take the king at once because he did not know whether to return a heart or a diamond. He hoped to get a signal from West on the next club play.

Declarer now led the nine of clubs and West had to decide on a discard. He had an unpleasant choice. He was afraid to discard the six of diamonds for fear East might read it as a signal showing the ace. He was also afraid to discard the three of hearts, even though it constituted a signal, because his partner might not realize that he had a lower heart.

West finally decided to throw the three of hearts. Declarer thereupon repeated the club finesse which East took with the king. Misinterpreting the heart discard, East returned a diamond and South wound up making three notrump instead of going down three.

Actually the problem that arose could have been solved on an entirely different basis. If East-West had been familiar with the suit-direction convention, they would have had no trouble defeating the contract.

According to this convention, West's return of his highest spade, the ten, showed an entry in the higher-ranking suit (as between hearts and diamonds). If West had had the ace of diamonds, he would have returned the five of spades instead. A high card calls for the high suit; a low card for the low suit.

The Only Chance

North dealer.
Neither side vulnerable.

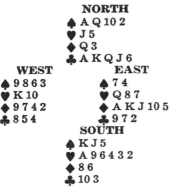

NORTH
♠ A Q 10 2
♥ J 5
♦ Q 3
♣ A K Q J 6

WEST
♠ 9 8 6 3
♥ K 10
♦ 9 7 4 2
♣ 8 5 4

EAST
♠ 7 4
♥ Q 8 7
♦ A K J 10 5
♣ 9 7 2

SOUTH
♠ K J 5
♥ A 9 6 4 3 2
♦ 8 6
♣ 10 3

The bidding:

North	East	South	West
1 ♣	1 ♦	1 ♥	Pass
1 ♠	Pass	2 ♥	Pass
4 ♥			

Opening lead—two of diamonds.

It is a basic rule that if there is only one distribution of the adverse cards that permits you to make the contract, you play for that distribution to exist. It cannot be right to concede defeat if there is any possibility of avoiding it.

South was in four hearts and West led a diamond. East cashed two diamonds and for want of anything better to do continued the suit. Declarer ruffed it in his hand and was now faced with the problem of losing only one trump trick.

Obviously, the contract could not be made if the trumps were divided 4-1 or 5-0. So declarer had to start on the basis that the trumps were divided 3-2.

Declarer also realized that against most 3-2 divisions of the trump suit he would be defeated regardless of how he handled the hearts. So in order to make the hand he had to assume the existence of only those 3-2 divisions of hearts that would allow him to escape with one trump loser against the best defense.

Of these, there were only two cases possible that would permit him to make the contract. Only if West had the K-10 or Q-10 of hearts alone could the hand be made.

Accordingly, after ruffing the diamond, South led a low heart. It did not matter what West did at this point. If he played the ten, dummy's jack would force the queen. Whatever East returned, South could then cash the ace to drop the king and next capture East's eight with the nine.

And if West took the first heart lead with the king (which is what he actually did), the defense was equally in bad shape. When West took the king and returned a spade, declarer won it in dummy and played the jack of hearts.

When East ducked, South finessed and thus held himself to one trump loser. If East had covered, the result would have been the same.

Of course, South was lucky to make the hand, but he earned what he got by capitalizing on his one chance.

A Small Investment Brings a Large Profit

South dealer.
North-South vulnerable.

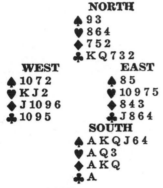

NORTH
♠ 9 3
♥ 8 6 4
♦ 7 5 2
♣ K Q 7 3 2

WEST
♠ 10 7 2
♥ K J 2
♦ J 10 9 6
♣ 10 9 5

EAST
♠ 8 5
♥ 10 9 7 5
♦ 8 4 3
♣ J 8 6 4

SOUTH
♠ A K Q J 6 4
♥ A Q 3
♦ A K Q
♣ A

The bidding:

South	West	North	East
2 ♠	Pass	2 NT	Pass
3 ♠	Pass	4 ♠	Pass
6 ♠			

Opening lead—jack of diamonds.

If you concede a trick you don't have to lose but get back two in exchange, you naturally show a profit for the transaction.

The sacrifice play doesn't come up very often, but when it does, it is sometimes overlooked. The reason is chiefly psychological, since it isn't normal to deliberately lose a trick you can win.

Take this hand where South contracted for six spades. West led a diamond which declarer took with the ace. Declarer drew trumps and eventually played the ace and a low heart, hoping the king would fall.

When it didn't, South went down one.

Actually, South had a much better chance of making the hand by a play that did not depend on the luck of finding either opponent with the singleton or doubleton king of hearts. (There was only about a 10% likelihood that the East-West cards would be divided in this way.)

What South should have done was cash the ace of clubs at trick two and then play a low spade towards the nine. The cards being distributed the way they were, this play would have made the contract.

West could do no better than take his ten of spades and return a diamond, but South could then enter dummy with a trump and discard two hearts on the K-Q of clubs.

Declarer should reason that there is a 50% chance of finding West with the ten of spades and that the slam is likely to be made if this is the case.

He should be willing to sacrifice a trump trick in order to try to reach dummy to obtain two valuable discards on the K-Q of clubs. He may go down an extra trick if it turns out that East has the ten of spades, but this is a relatively minor loss to suffer alongside the gain he can show if West has the ten.

Declarer has a lot to win and only a little to lose by this method of play.

Concealing
Your
Intentions

South dealer.
North-South vulnerable.

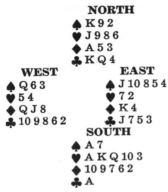

NORTH
♠ K 9 2
♥ J 9 8 6
♦ A 5 3
♣ K Q 4

WEST
♠ Q 6 3
♥ 5 4
♦ Q J 8
♣ 10 9 8 6 2

EAST
♠ J 10 8 5 4
♥ 7 2
♦ K 4
♣ J 7 5 3

SOUTH
♠ A 7
♥ A K Q 10 3
♦ 10 9 7 6 2
♣ A

The bidding:

South	West	North	East
1 ♥	Pass	3 ♥	Pass
6 ♥			

Opening lead—ten of clubs.

The day may come, though I doubt it, when bidding will be so scientific that everybody will always get to the right contract. But until that day comes, if it ever does, we'll just have to struggle along with certain difficult hands, trying to salvage what we can from the bad contracts all of us occasionally get to.

You can criticize the bidding in this hand if you want to, but the fact is that many a good pair would wind up in the same bad contract with two diamond losers. The K-Q of clubs are wasted values for North to hold opposite the South hand.

If North had had the king, queen, or jack of diamonds in place of the K-Q of clubs, the slam would have been a satisfactory one. But, things being the way they were, the contract was a poor one.

However, South made the slam anyway. He recognized that normal play was not apt to succeed and that the only real chance of making the hand was to find either defender with the K-x of diamonds alone.

So, after winning the club lead with the ace, he played a low diamond to the ace at trick two, both opponents following low. He then drew two rounds of trumps, cashed the K-Q of clubs and A-K of spades, and ruffed a spade.

When he now led a diamond, East was forced to win with the king and return either a spade or a club. This gave South a ruff and discard and he made the slam as a result.

Of course, East could have defeated the contract by dropping the king of diamonds on the ace when it was played. Probably, he would have done this if South had telegraphed his intentions by first clearing the hearts, clubs and spades before tackling the diamond suit. But the play of the diamond ace so early in the hand made it difficult for East to realize exactly what South was up to, and, eventually, it cost him the contract.

The King
Can Do
No Wrong

South dealer.
Both sides vulnerable.

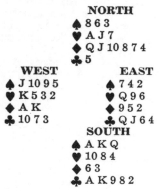

NORTH
- ♠ 8 6 3
- ♥ A J 7
- ♦ Q J 10 8 7 4
- ♣ 5

WEST
- ♠ J 10 9 5
- ♥ K 5 3 2
- ♦ A K
- ♣ 10 7 3

EAST
- ♠ 7 4 2
- ♥ Q 9 6
- ♦ 9 5 2
- ♣ Q J 6 4

SOUTH
- ♠ A K Q
- ♥ 10 8 4
- ♦ 6 3
- ♣ A K 9 8 2

The bidding:

South	West	North	East
1 ♣	Pass	1 ♦	Pass
2 ♣	Pass	2 ♦	Pass
2 NT	Pass	3 NT	

Opening lead—jack of spades.

Let's say you have the West hand and lead a spade against three notrump. Declarer wins the jack with the ace, and the first thing you do is make a mental note that South has the A-K-Q.

You don't actually see the A-K-Q, but your partner's deuce is highly illuminating. He wouldn't play the two if he had the K-Q-2 because he would want to encourage the continuation of the suit (by playing the queen), nor would he play the two with the Q-7-2 for the same reason (he would play the seven in such case).

South now leads a diamond, which you take with the king—partner again playing the two. Here you make a note also that East started with three diamonds. It would be his duty, if he had only two of them, to start a high-low in order to give you a count on how many diamonds declarer started with.

It is now your play and the crucial point of the hand has been reached. There is only one proper play to beat the hand—the king of hearts—but let's examine the evidence to see why you should make this startling but necessary play.

If you stand pat by leading another spade, you know what will happen. South will win and return a diamond to establish dummy's long suit, and that is sure to prove fatal.

You can't afford to be idle at a time like this. You must try to destroy the value of dummy's diamonds by attacking dummy's entry. There is a good chance that East has the queen of hearts, considering the bidding. If that is the case, dummy's diamonds are dead.

Remember that South is known to have club strength, having bid the suit twice, and also the A-K-Q of spades. At the same time you say to yourself that if South has the queen of hearts nothing can help you regardless of what you do, so you might as well make a try at beating the hand.

The king can do no wrong!

Quest For a Queen

West dealer.
East-West vulnerable.

```
                    NORTH
                 ♠ A 10 7 4
                 ♥ A 9 8
                 ♦ A J
                 ♣ 9 7 6 2
     WEST                      EAST
  ♠ Q 5 3                   ♠ J 9 6
  ♥ Q 6 2                   ♥ 5 3
  ♦ Q 8 4                   ♦ 10 7 6 3 2
  ♣ A K Q 10                ♣ 8 5 4
                    SOUTH
                 ♠ K 8 2
                 ♥ K J 10 7 4
                 ♦ K 9 5
                 ♣ J 3
```

The bidding:

West	North	East	South
1 ♣	Dble.	Pass	2 ♥
Pass	3 ♥	Pass	4 ♥

Opening lead—king of clubs.

It is sometimes possible to solve a pressing problem by running away from it. South more or less did that in this hand where he was declarer at four hearts.

West led the king of clubs and continued with the ace and queen, South ruffing the third club. Since he had already lost two tricks and was practically sure to lose a spade trick also, South's problem was to try to escape a trump loser.

He could not be sure of the location of the queen of hearts, so, instead of trying to guess which way to finesse against the missing queen, he adopted a course of play designed to avoid the possibility of misguessing the trump situation.

He cashed the A-K of diamonds and then trumped a diamond in dummy. Next he played a spade to the king and a spade back to the ace. When he then ruffed dummy's last club, he was left with four cards, consisting of the eight of spades and the K-J-10 of hearts.

At this point it did not matter which opponent had the queen of hearts, since he was now bound to make three of the last four tricks. He led a spade and could then afford to sit back and relax.

As it happened, West won the trick with the queen and was forced to return a heart, thus solving declarer's problem of escaping a trump loser, but it would not have mattered if East had been able to win the spade trick. In that case, East would have been on lead, and whatever card he returned, South could play the ten of hearts and thus be sure to smother the queen, whether it was held by East or West.

It could be argued that on the bidding West was very likely to have been dealt the queen of hearts and that South could therefore have accomplished the same result by finessing through him. However, this method of play was not nearly as likely to succeed as the method declarer actually adopted.

A Cooked Goose

South dealer.
North-South vulnerable.

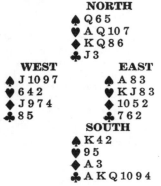

NORTH
♠ Q 6 5
♥ A Q 10 7
♦ K Q 8 6
♣ J 3

WEST
♠ J 10 9 7
♥ 6 4 2
♦ J 9 7 4
♣ 8 5

EAST
♠ A 8 3
♥ K J 8 3
♦ 10 5 2
♣ 7 6 2

SOUTH
♠ K 4 2
♥ 9 5
♦ A 3
♣ A K Q 10 9 4

The bidding:

South	West	North	East
1 ♣	Pass	1 ♥	Pass
3 ♣	Pass	3 ♦	Pass
3 NT	Pass	6 NT	Dble.

Once upon a time there lived a mule who refused to learn anything at all about conventions. He thought conventions were strictly for the birds.

One day the mule (who *always* sat West) was playing in a small-steak game with a mongoose. Now the mongoose was certainly not the best player in the animal kingdom, but he did know a thing or two about conventions. He used to read every bridge book and magazine he could lay his paws on.

In this hand, their opponents —an owl (who sat South) and a pussycat (who sat North)— got to six notrump on the bidding sequence shown. The mongoose, thoroughly familiar with the slam-doubling convention, doubled when the pussycat bid six notrump.

He knew that the double, in a slam contract, called for partner to lead the first suit bid by dummy. The mongoose was confident that a heart lead would beat the slam.

However, the mule was accustomed to leading the jack of spades with his kind of hand, so he naturally led the jack of spades. He knew he was supposed to lead a heart on the bidding, but, being a very stubborn critter, he wouldn't do it. He wasn't going to be swayed by any newfangled conventions, regardless of what anyone said.

The owl played low from the pussycat's hand and the mongoose played low also. (If the mongoose had taken the ace, South would have had twelve easy tricks.)

The owl won the spade with the king, and, being a wise old owl, he knew the mongoose had doubled the slam because he had the king of hearts as well as the ace of spades and wanted a heart lead. So the owl cashed the A-K-Q of diamonds and six club tricks, reducing the pussycat's hand to the queen of spades and the A-Q of hearts.

The mongoose's last three cards consisted of the ace of spades and K-J of hearts.

The owl then blinked knowingly and led a spade, and the mongoose's goose was cooked!

A Problem in Probabilities

South dealer.
Neither side vulnerable.

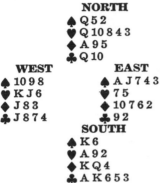

NORTH
♠ Q 5 2
♥ Q 10 8 4 3
♦ A 9 5
♣ Q 10

WEST
♠ 10 9 8
♥ K J 6
♦ J 8 3
♣ J 8 7 4

EAST
♠ A J 7 4 3
♥ 7 5
♦ 10 7 6 2
♣ 9 2

SOUTH
♠ K 6
♥ A 9 2
♦ K Q 4
♣ A K 6 5 3

The bidding:

South	West	North	East
1 ♣	Pass	1 ♥	Pass
2 NT	Pass	3 NT	

Opening lead—ten of spades.

Which suit to attack and when and how to attack it determines the result of many a hand. Declarer cannot properly make a decision in such a case until after he has weighed all the evidence and considered the course of play most likely to succeed.

South is in three notrump and West opens a spade. Declarer ducks in dummy and wins with the king. The question is whether he should now lead hearts or clubs.

There are several ways for South to play the hand. He can begin by cashing three rounds of clubs, and if he finds the suit divided 3-3, he will coast in with ten tricks. Or, if he finds the clubs divided 4-2, with East having the four, he can then give East a club trick and thus build his fifth club into a guaranteed ninth trick.

But if, after three rounds of clubs, declarer learns that West started with four clubs, he may find himself in a peck of trouble. To give up a club at this point would put West on lead, and this could prove fatal if West returned a spade and it turned out that East had the spade length and strength.

Alternatively, South can begin the play of the hand by attacking hearts immediately—for example, by leading the ace and another heart. This line of play, however, is subject to the objection just mentioned—West may obtain the lead and return a spade.

The proper play, all things considered, is for South to lead a club towards dummy at trick two and finesse the ten. This play guarantees the contract whenever West has the jack and also wins the hand whenever West has two, three or four clubs of any denomination.

For practical purposes, the first round club finesse assures the contract. It can lose only when West was dealt a singleton club or x-x-x-x-x of clubs, and must win in all other cases. In the actual hand, the club finesse results in declarer's making ten tricks, whereas almost any other line of play would lead to defeat.

Stop and Think

South dealer.
Neither side vulnerable.

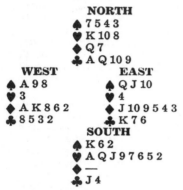

NORTH
♠ 7 5 4 3
♥ K 10 8
♦ Q 7
♣ A Q 10 9

WEST
♠ A 9 8
♥ 3
♦ A K 8 6 2
♣ 8 5 3 2

EAST
♠ Q J 10
♥ 4
♦ J 10 9 5 4 3
♣ K 7 6

SOUTH
♠ K 6 2
♥ A Q J 9 7 6 5 2
♦ —
♣ J 4

The bidding:

South	West	North	East
4 ♥	Pass	Pass	Pass

Opening lead — king of diamonds.

Here is the kind of hand it would be easy for anyone to misplay. There is no doubt that some plays in bridge are not altogether obvious, even though they are clearly correct, and this hand contains one that might easily be missed.

South was in four hearts and West led the king of diamonds. Declarer ruffed, drew a round of trump, and led the jack of clubs and finessed. East took the king, returned the queen of spades, and South went down one, losing three spades and a club.

There is no doubt that South was unlucky to find East with the king of clubs and West with the ace of spades. Nevertheless, he should have made the hand. He should have taken out insurance to guard against these possibilities.

The method of play that practically guarantees the contract is to discard a club on the opening lead of the king of diamonds. It does not matter in the actual hand what West plays next, but let's assume he continues with the ace of diamonds.

The contract is now 100 per cent sure. Declarer draws a round of trump (two, if necessary) and plays the jack of clubs to the ace. Then he leads the queen of clubs.

If East has the king and covers, South ruffs and enters dummy with a trump to discard two spades on the 10-9 of clubs. If East does not cover the queen, South discards a spade and continues with the ten of clubs. He is assured of eleven tricks if East has the king of clubs.

If West has the king, South is still sure of the contract. When he leads the queen of clubs and discards a spade, West can win with the king, but that does not prevent South from winning ten tricks. In fact, if West does not cash the ace of spades at this point, declarer makes five odd.

The key to the hand is the play at trick one.

Rising to the Occasion

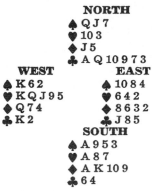

South dealer.
Both sides vulnerable.

```
                NORTH
              ♠ Q J 7
              ♥ 10 3
              ♦ J 5
              ♣ A Q 10 9 7 3
  WEST                    EAST
♠ K 6 2               ♠ 10 8 4
♥ K Q J 9 5           ♥ 6 4 2
♦ Q 7 4               ♦ 8 6 3 2
♣ K 2                 ♣ J 8 5
                SOUTH
              ♠ A 9 5 3
              ♥ A 8 7
              ♦ A K 10 9
              ♣ 6 4
```

The bidding:

South	West	North	East
1 ♦	1 ♥	2 ♣	Pass
2 NT	Pass	3 NT	

Opening lead—king of hearts.

Let's say you have the West hand and are defending against three notrump. You lead the king of hearts, of course, and, after dummy comes down, you have mixed feelings about the contract.

Having the guarded king of spades and queen of diamonds behind declarer gives you some feeling of comfort, but this is largely negated by the threatening clubs in dummy. You see that declarer can score six club tricks in dummy if he has any three clubs, or the J-x, or even the singleton jack. And you can also be sure that if he makes six club tricks he makes the contract.

Of course, it's possible your partner has three clubs to the jack, in which case declarer can't make six club tricks. In that case, he would be able to make only five club tricks after finessing the nine and losing to the jack. But even five club tricks figure to make the contract for South.

All these thoughts, and more, occur to you when you lead the king of hearts, the queen, and next the jack, which South finally takes with the ace. And then, as expected, South plays a club, intending to double-finesse and thus make the contract.

But if you're on your toes, you play the king, and no sooner do you do this than South's house of cards collapses. He can't afford to let the king win because you'd cash your hearts to defeat the contract, so he therefore takes the king with the ace.

And then, no matter which way he turns, he goes down. Whether he now chooses to finesse a spade or a diamond, or return to his hand to play a club and possibly finesse, makes little difference.

The up-with-the-king play stops declarer stone-cold dead. It leaves him without resource. But if you play low on the club when South leads the suit at trick four, he makes at least nine tricks by playing the nine from dummy.

More About Queens

South dealer.
Both sides vulnerable.

```
                    NORTH
                 ♠ A K 10 3
                 ♥ Q 5
                 ♦ Q 9 8 7
                 ♣ K 10 8
        WEST                 EAST
     ♠ Q 8 7 4             ♠ J 9 5 2
     ♥ A K J 10 6 3        ♥ 9 2
     ♦ 6 2                 ♦ 5 3
     ♣ 4                   ♣ Q 7 6 3 2
                    SOUTH
                 ♠ 6
                 ♥ 8 7 4
                 ♦ A K J 10 4
                 ♣ A J 9 5
```

The bidding:

South	West	North	East
1 ♦	1 ♥	1 ♠	Pass
2 ♣	Pass	3 ♦	Pass
4 ♦	Pass	5 ♦	

Opening lead—king of hearts.

Two-way finesses for a missing queen are the bane of many a bridge player's existence, but they're not as difficult to handle as they're cracked up to be.

The declarer can usually find a way of guessing correctly if he puts his mind to the subject. There are nearly always enough clues around to point the way to where the queen is located, and all that declarer has to do is gather up these clues to reach the right conclusion.

Let's say you've reached five diamonds on the bidding shown and West cashes the A-K of hearts and continues with the jack. You ruff in dummy, East throwing a club, and there you are, sure to make the hand if only you knew which opponent had the queen of clubs.

The queen is finessable all right, whether East or West has the damsel, but which way to finesse—through East or West—is the vital question. You don't solve such problems by mentally tossing a coin—there's much more to it than that. Instead, you first try to find out as much about the opponents' hands as you can.

You've already learned one important thing—that West started with six hearts and East with two. If you could only find out how the spades and diamonds were divided, you'd be in a much better position to deal with the clubs.

So you start out by cashing the ace of spades and trumping a spade. Then you draw two rounds of trumps ending in dummy. In the process you discover that the diamonds were divided 2-2. Now you cash the king of spades, discarding a club, and then you ruff the ten of spades, learning that the spades were divided 4-4.

The picture is complete. West started with exactly four spades, six hearts and two diamonds. He therefore has precisely one club—neither more nor less. So you play a club to the king and a club back. When East follows low, you finesse, knowing positively that the finesse will succeed.

The Safety Factor

North dealer.
North-South vulnerable.

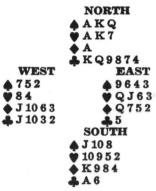

```
                    NORTH
                 ♠ A K Q
                 ♥ A K 7
                 ♦ A
                 ♣ K Q 9 8 7 4
      WEST                      EAST
   ♠ 7 5 2                   ♠ 9 6 4 3
   ♥ 8 4                     ♥ Q J 6 3
   ♦ J 10 6 3                ♦ Q 7 5 2
   ♣ J 10 3 2                ♣ 5
                    SOUTH
                 ♠ J 10 8
                 ♥ 10 9 5 2
                 ♦ K 9 8 4
                 ♣ A 6
```

The bidding:

North	East	South	West
2 ♣	Pass	2 NT	Pass
3 ♣	Pass	4 NT	Pass
6 NT			

Opening lead—three of diamonds.

The declarer has to be on his toes when he plays a contract which might be defeated if the adverse cards are unfavorably divided. It is useless to attribute a poor result to bad luck after the hand is over, if the declarer can cater to the possibility of a bad lie of the cards.

South became declarer at six notrump and West led a diamond.

South went blithely ahead, saying he would probably make seven. He took the ace of diamonds, played a club to the ace, and then cashed the king of diamonds, discarding a heart from dummy.

When he then played a club to the queen and East showed out, the hand was over. He went down two for minus 200, when he could have scored a plus of 1,640 points with proper play.

In hands like this the declarer should say to himself at the start: "What can defeat me?" It is quite obvious that thirteen tricks are there for the asking if the clubs are divided 3-2, as they are most of the time.

What declarer should do is assume that the clubs are divided 4-1 and then look for some way to cope with that division if it exists. To barge ahead in the expectation of a 3-2 break, without attempting to protect against a worse division, is a style of play that will many times produce disastrous results.

The proper play in this case is to lead a club from dummy at trick two and finesse the six. Once West follows suit, the contract is sure to make.

By playing in this fashion, South caters to the possible 4-1 club division, and puts himself in the position where he retains the ace of clubs so that he does not have to cash the king of diamonds prematurely.

This safety play may cost him a 30-point trick (if the clubs are divided 3-2), but that is a very small premium to pay for slam insurance.

Super Defense

East dealer.
Both sides vulnerable.

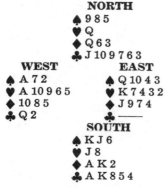

```
                    NORTH
                    ♠ 9 8 5
                    ♥ Q
                    ♦ Q 6 3
                    ♣ J 10 9 7 6 3
        WEST                    EAST
        ♠ A 7 2                 ♠ Q 10 4 3
        ♥ A 10 9 6 5            ♥ K 7 4 3 2
        ♦ 10 8 5               ♦ J 9 7 4
        ♣ Q 2                  ♣ ——
                    SOUTH
                    ♠ K J 6
                    ♥ J 8
                    ♦ A K 2
                    ♣ A K 8 5 4
```

The bidding:

East	South	West	North
Pass	1 ♣	1 ♥	Pass
4 ♥	Pass	Pass	5 ♣
Pass	Pass	Dble.	

Opening lead—ace of hearts.

Defense is sometimes a delicate proposition. Look at this hand where West had to measure the situation perfectly to defeat five clubs.

South might have doubled four hearts, and this contract would have been defeated if North had accepted the double.

West led the ace of hearts against five clubs and shifted to a low diamond. Declarer won the trick with the king, ruffed a heart, and then cashed the A-K of clubs and A-Q of diamonds, ending in dummy.

He had eliminated all red cards from his own hand and dummy's by this time and was ready to tackle spades. To make the contract he had to hold himself to one spade loser.

He led the nine of spades. If East had ducked, South would have made the contract by playing low from his hand. But East rose to the occasion and played the ten on the nine.

South covered with the jack and now it was West who had to come through with the right play. He let the jack hold, playing the deuce. As a result, South had to go down one.

Declarer entered dummy with a trump in order to lead another spade, but it did not matter whether he led the eight or five from dummy. In either case, he was bound to lose two spades and go down. Thus, if he led the eight, East would cover with the queen, while if he led the five, East would play low to trap the king.

But suppose West had taken the jack of spades with the ace when the suit was first led. Then he could not have defeated the contract regardless of what he returned.

If he led back the seven, dummy would play the eight to trap East's queen, while if he led back the deuce, dummy would play low to again trap the queen.

West's lowly seven proved to be the key factor in the razor-sharp battle.

Snatching Defeat
From the
Jaws of Victory

East dealer.
East-West vulnerable.

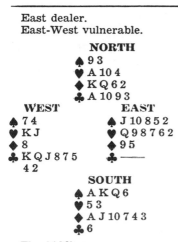

                    NORTH
                    ♠ 9 3
                    ♥ A 10 4
                    ♦ K Q 6 2
                    ♣ A 10 9 3
WEST   **EAST**
♠ 7 4   ♠ J 10 8 5 2
♥ K J   ♥ Q 9 8 7 6 2
♦ 8   ♦ 9 5
♣ K Q J 8 7 5   ♣ —
4 2
                    SOUTH
                    ♠ A K Q 6
                    ♥ 5 3
                    ♦ A J 10 7 4 3
                    ♣ 6

The bidding:

East	South	West	North
Pass	1 ♦	2 ♣	Dble.
2 ♥	2 ♠	Pass	3 ♥
Pass	4 ♦	Pass	5 ♣
Pass	5 ♠	Pass	6 ♦

Opening lead—king of clubs.

You have to train yourself not to make mechanical plays in bridge if you expect to get the best results.

Here is a hand that illustrates the point. It was played in a par bridge contest that is staged annually among representatives of the Department of State in various legations, embassies and other foreign offices all over the globe. Usually, close to 2,000 persons compete in these contests.

North-South were supposed to bid and make six diamonds to earn full par. The bidding shown is merely one sequence that might be used to arrive at the sound contract of six dia- monds. Failure to reach a slam was punished with an under-par bidding score.

The directed opening lead was the king of clubs. Most of the contestants who became de- clarer at six diamonds met their Waterloo on the first trick. They played the ace of clubs, which East ruffed, and even- tually lost a heart trick to go down one.

With proper play, they would have made the slam. All they had to do to assure twelve tricks was play a low club from dummy on the opening lead. This somewhat unusual play was clearly called for by the circumstances.

South can see twelve tricks as soon as dummy comes down. They consist of three high spades and a spade ruff, the ace of hearts, the ace of clubs, and six trump tricks. The only thing that South has to guard against is the loss of one of those winners.

Playing the ace of clubs at trick one jeopardizes the con- tract. True, the play will lose only if West has an eight-card suit, but that possibility is far from remote in the light of the bidding.

Even if it is granted that East is unlikely to trump the ace of clubs, there can still be no advantage to playing the ace. The duck guarantees the contract; the ace play jeopar- dizes it.

If West continues with the queen, dummy ducks again to assure the slam.

Waiting
for a
Signal

North dealer.
Both sides vulnerable.

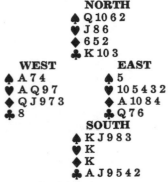

NORTH
♠ Q 10 6 2
♥ J 8 6
♦ 6 5 2
♣ K 10 3

WEST
♠ A 7 4
♥ A Q 9 7
♦ Q J 9 7 3
♣ 8

EAST
♠ 5
♥ 10 5 4 3 2
♦ A 10 8 4
♣ Q 7 6

SOUTH
♠ K J 9 8 3
♥ K
♦ K
♣ A J 9 5 4 2

The bidding:

North	East	South	West
Pass	Pass	1 ♠	Dble
2 ♠	3 ♥	4 ♠	Dble

Opening lead—eight of clubs.

"Dear Mr. Becker: This deal occurred in a friendly team of four match I recently played in, and it has been bothering me ever since because I was entirely responsible for a huge swing against my team.

"I held the West cards and, whether you agree with my bidding or not, the fact is that South became declarer at four spades doubled.

"I led my singleton club and South, who had never mentioned his clubs, played the ten from dummy, East and South following low. Declarer continued with a low trump and I won his king with the ace.

"It was at this point that I made a terribly expensive play. It seemed to me that my partner would surely have the king of hearts for his three heart bid, so I returned a low heart on the assumption that when he won with the king he would realize that my purpose in underleading the ace was to get a club ruff.

"Unfortunately, S o u t h produced the king and the outcome was that he made the contract with two overtricks for a score of 1,190 points. Had I known to lead a diamond at trick three, we would have put declarer down one for a score of 200 points.

"Was my heart play really as bad as the result seems to indicate? Sorrowfully yours, Constant Reader."

Dear C. R.: No it wasn't, but you did make a serious mistake a trick earlier when you won the king of spades with the ace. It would have been wiser to duck the king, win the next trump lead, and make your next play in accordance with East's discard on the ace of spades.

In the a c t u a l hand, East would have discarded either the deuce of hearts to stop you from leading a heart, or a high diamond to get you to lead a diamond. Either way, you could then have beaten the contract by leading a diamond to partner's ace and getting a club ruff.

The Grand Slam Force

South dealer.
Neither side vulnerable.

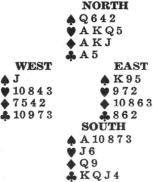

NORTH
♠ Q 6 4 2
♥ A K Q 5
♦ A K J
♣ A 5

WEST
♠ J
♥ 10 8 4 3
♦ 7 5 4 2
♣ 10 9 7 3

EAST
♠ K 9 5
♥ 9 7 2
♦ 10 8 6 3
♣ 8 6 2

SOUTH
♠ A 10 8 7 3
♥ J 6
♦ Q 9
♣ K Q J 4

The bidding:

South	West	North	East
1 ♠	Pass	3 ♥	Pass
3 ♠	Pass	4 NT	Pass
5 ♦	Pass	5 NT	Pass
6 ♦	Pass	7 ♠	

Opening lead—ten of clubs.

The grand slam force is a convention not widely known and seldom used, but it can prove very effective on the rare occasions when it does arise.

Suppose partner opened the bidding with a spade and you held the North hand. Naturally, you would feel confident of a small slam and would be wondering whether or not you had a grand slam.

You would bid the grand slam if you knew positively that your partner's spade suit included the A-K, but you might be afraid to undertake it for fear he was lacking the king or the ace.

That's where the grand slam force comes in. You find out, by using the convention, whether or not partner has these key cards.

The way it works is this. You jump to five notrump over one spade—or, if you've bid three hearts and partner three spades, you then bid five notrump.

This requests partner to bid seven spades if he has two of the three top trump honors (that is, A-K, A-Q, or K-Q). If he does not have them, he simply bids six spades.

The convention would have come in handy in this deal and kept South out of a bad contract. North would have learned that the opponents had either the ace or king of spades and would have stopped at six. Using Blackwood, which he did, he discovered that South had either the king of spades or king of clubs, but not knowing which, he decided to gamble it was the king of spades.

Luckily, South made the contract even though he had the wrong king. He won the club lead in dummy and played the queen of spades. East covered with the king—it would not have mattered if he had ducked —and South took the ace, catching the jack. A later trump finesse trapped East's nine.

Note that the only combination of cards which permits South to avoid a spade loser is the case where West has precisely the singleton jack. Declarer played for this one possibility—and succeeded.

The Art of Deception

South dealer.
North-South vulnerable.

```
              NORTH
              ♠ 7 6 4
              ♥ A 5 3
              ♦ K J
              ♣ A 10 8 7 2
WEST                      EAST
♠ K Q 10 9 8             ♠ 5 3
♥ K Q 10                 ♥ J 9 8 4
♦ 10 7 5                 ♦ 9 6 4 3 2
♣ 6 3                    ♣ K 4
              SOUTH
              ♠ A J 2
              ♥ 7 6 2
              ♦ A Q 8
              ♣ Q J 9 5
```

The bidding:

South	West	North	East
1 ♣	1 ♠	3 ♣	Pass
3 NT			

Opening lead—king of spades.

The art of falsecarding is a study in itself. Most types of falsecards repeat themselves often and are well known to the experienced player, but there are many falsecards that are not so well known to the everyday player.

Here is a fine example of an imaginative play that resulted in declarer's making a contract otherwise doomed to defeat. South was in three notrump and West led the king of spades.

It was clear to declarer that the contract could be made if West had the king of clubs. In such case he could bring home five club tricks and make at least four notrump.

South therefore had to play on the basis that East had the king of clubs and at the same time take every conceivable precaution to guard against that possibility.

Declarer saw that if he captured the king of spades with the ace and took a club finesse, he would very likely be defeated by a spade return if the finesse lost.

He likewise realized that if he played the deuce on the king of spades, West would probably shift to hearts rather than continue with spades in the face of East's play of the discouraging three.

In the actual hand, if South had played low, West would no doubt have attacked hearts, and whether or not dummy took the ace immediately, South would have gone down.

Appreciating the danger of playing the ace and the futility of playing the deuce, South came forth instead with the startling play of the jack!

This falsecard had the intended effect. West naturally assumed that South had the A-J alone and continued with the queen. Declarer won it with the ace, led the queen of clubs, and finessed.

East took the king, but could return nothing to prevent South from cashing nine tricks. He had no more spades to lead, but even if East had had another spade to play, South would still have been on solid ground because West, in that case, would have only two more spades to cash.

Subtle Defense

South dealer.
East-West vulnerable.

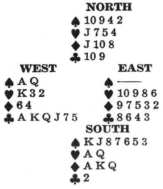

```
                    NORTH
                 ♠ 10 9 4 2
                 ♥ J 7 5 4
                 ♦ J 10 8
                 ♣ 10 9
    WEST                       EAST
 ♠ A Q                      ♠ ———
 ♥ K 3 2                    ♥ 10 9 8 6
 ♦ 6 4                      ♦ 9 7 5 3 2
 ♣ A K Q J 7 5              ♣ 8 6 4 3
                    SOUTH
                 ♠ K J 8 7 6 5 3
                 ♥ A Q
                 ♦ A K Q
                 ♣ 2
```

The bidding:

South	West	North	East
1 ♠	Dble.	Pass	2 ♦
3 ♠	3 NT	4 ♠	

Opening lead—king of clubs.

Defensive play does not have to be dramatic to be good. Here is an example of excellent defense, the kind that passes unnoticed until attention is drawn to it.

South and West each had 19 high-card points, but South eventually became declarer at four spades.

West led the king of clubs and shifted to a diamond at trick two. Declarer won with the queen, and having nothing better to play, led a spade.

West cashed both his trumps and then led the ace of clubs. Declarer ruffed, but later went down one because he had to lose a heart to the king.

What's remarkable about the defense, you may ask? Well, let's see what would have happened if West had not led a diamond at trick two. Suppose he had continued with a club, as most players would.

South ruffs, but now has the contract in tow. It is not hard for him to deduce from the bidding that West has the A-Q of spades. Therefore, in order to avoid staking the result of the contract on a heart finesse, he decides to endplay West.

Since the North-South hands are already out of clubs, declarer arranges to run both hands out of diamonds. He leads the A-K-Q of diamonds.

West can ruff the last diamond if he wants to, but it would put him on lead with no safe exit card. So let's suppose he discards on the third diamond.

This does not allow him to escape his fate, however, because South now plays a trump to saddle West with the lead. West cashes the A-Q, but is then in a losing position.

He must either return a heart into declarer's A-Q, or play a club which permits South to discard a heart as the club is ruffed in dummy.

West's farsighted diamond play at trick two prevents all this from happening. It forestalls the endplay that would otherwise take place. It stops the declarer stone-cold dead.

How Would You Play This One?

West dealer.
Both sides vulnerable.

```
                NORTH
                ♠ A Q 9 3
                ♥ 8 3
                ♦ J 9
                ♣ 9 7 6 5 2
   WEST                      EAST
♠ J 8 6                      ♠ K 10 5 4 2
♥ K 7                        ♥ 4
♦ A 5 3 2                    ♦ K 10 8 7
♣ Q J 10 3                   ♣ K 8 4
                SOUTH
                ♠ 7
                ♥ A Q J 10 9 6 5 2
                ♦ Q 6 4
                ♣ A
```

The bidding:

West	North	East	South
Pass	Pass	Pass	4 ♥

Opening lead—queen of clubs.

Your batting average as declarer would rise appreciably if you could actually see how the defenders' cards are divided instead of having to guess the distribution of their high cards and their suits.

However, there are some hands that are troublesome even when you see all 52 cards. Such hands are comparatively few and far between, but they do have some fascination when they arise.

You might want to try making four hearts with this hand, having the benefit of looking at the East-West cards. It may puzzle you for a while.

Probably the instinctive play, after winning the ace of clubs, is to lead a low diamond and finesse the nine when West plays low. This will not work in the present hand because East would win with the ten and return a trump. Eventually you would lose three diamonds and a heart to go down one.

The same result would probably be obtained if you played the jack instead of the nine.

The best way of playing the hand is to enter dummy at trick two with a spade and lead the nine of diamonds. If East follows low, so do you, and your troubles are over. But if, as is likely, East covers with the ten, you play the queen. (It does not do East any good to go up with the king because all you would lose is two diamonds and a heart.)

West takes the ace, but is stymied. He cannot afford to lead a trump, so let's say he returns a club. You ruff it and lead another diamond. East wins with the king and returns a trump.

Naturally, you refuse to finesse because that would jeopardize the contract. You take the heart with the ace, ruff your last diamond, and thus make four.

Actually, this line of play is best even if the East-West cards are not known, but it is very hard in actual practice to resist leading diamonds originally from the South hand.

One in a Million

East dealer.
Both sides vulnerable.

NORTH
♠ 6 5
♥ Q J 3 2
♦ Q 9
♣ Q 10 7 4 2

WEST
♠ A Q 4
♥ A 10 8 7
♦ K 6 5 3
♣ 6 5

EAST
♠ K 10 8 7 2
♥ 6 5
♦ 8 4
♣ A 9 8 3

SOUTH
♠ J 9 3
♥ K 9 4
♦ A J 10 7 2
♣ K J

The bidding:

East	South	West	North
Pass	1 ♦	Pass	1 ♥
Pass	1 NT		

Opening lead— six of clubs.

Here is one of the most unusual hands ever played in a world championship. It occurred in the U.S.-Thailand match during the 1964 Olympiad and featured one of the rarest plays in bridge — a double squeeze against declarer. Squeezes are almost invariably executed by the declarer, not by a defender.

The contract was one notrump played by Bob Hamman of the American team. West (Dr. M. Veeraburus) led a club. Dummy and East (B. Gimkiewicz) followed low and South won the first two tricks with the K-J of clubs.

Declarer led a heart to the jack, which held, and then finessed the queen of diamonds, which also held. Up to this point the defense had had four opportunities to win a trick and had rejected them all!

Declarer then tried another diamond finesse, but now the defense finally brought its guns into action and South never got another trick.

West won the diamond with the king and played the A-Q and another spade. East took the king and cashed the ten of spades and ace of clubs, at which point this became the position:

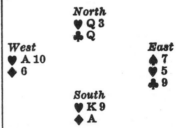

North
♥ Q 3
♣ Q

West
♥ A 10
♦ 6

East
♠ 7
♥ 5
♣ 9

South
♥ K 9
♦ A

Gimkiewicz cashed his last spade. South could not spare the ace of diamonds, which would make West's six a trick, so he discarded a heart.

When Dr. Veeraburus now discarded his diamond, dummy became squeezed in turn. To discard the queen of clubs would make East's nine a trick, so declarer was obliged to throw a heart from dummy.

As a result, West took the last two tricks with the A-10 of hearts and South went down three.

Playing on Air

South dealer.
Both sides vulnerable.

```
                NORTH
              ♠ A 6 4 3
              ♥ 9 6 2
              ♦ J 10 5 3
              ♣ J 4
   WEST                    EAST
♠ J 9                  ♠ K Q 10 8 7 2
♥ K J 10 8 4 3         ♥ Q 5
♦ 8 7 4               ♦ 9
♣ K 10                ♣ 9 8 7 2
                SOUTH
              ♠ 5
              ♥ A 7
              ♦ A K Q 6 2
              ♣ A Q 6 5 3
```

The bidding:

South	West	North	East
1 ♦	1 ♥	Pass	1 ♠
3 ♣	Pass	4 ♦	Pass
6 ♦			

Opening lead—jack of spades.

You shouldn't take a finesse just because the opportunity for it exists. There are times when it is better to concede a trick than try to save it. It's all a matter of the circumstances with which you're faced.

South was in six diamonds and West led a spade. It would seem to be natural to win the spade with the ace, take two rounds of trumps (three, if necessary) and then lead the jack of clubs from dummy and take a finesse when East plays low.

If you were to do this, you would find yourself going down one because you would lose a club trick and, later, a heart trick. True, you would make the hand if the clubs were divided 3-3 or the trumps 2-2, but, since they are not, you would wind up a trick short of the contract.

However, this would be the wrong way to play the hand. The chances of winning the club finesse are rather poor, considering the bidding that took place. East is marked with the K-Q of spades by the opening lead of the jack, and it is therefore reasonable to suppose that West's overcall is based on something more than just his heart suit.

The only value West can have outside of hearts is the king of clubs, and he should therefore be credited with it. Accordingly, the club finesse should be avoided.

Instead, South takes a third round of trump, after noting the 3-1 division, and leads a low club toward the jack. West is powerless against this play. The best he can do is take his king, dummy playing low of course. Then, whatever West returns, South can eventually discard dummy's hearts on the good clubs and thus make the slam.

The extra trick declarer gains on this line of play comes about because he forces West to play his king of clubs "on air," that is, West is compelled to win the club trick with the king while South contributes the three and dummy the four.

Sylvia
Rides
Again

South dealer.
Both sides vulnerable.

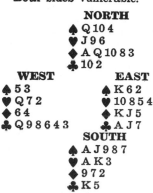

NORTH
- ♠ Q 10 4
- ♥ J 9 6
- ♦ A Q 10 8 3
- ♣ 10 2

WEST
- ♠ 5 3
- ♥ Q 7 2
- ♦ 6 4
- ♣ Q 9 8 6 4 3

EAST
- ♠ K 6 2
- ♥ 10 8 5 4
- ♦ K J 5
- ♣ A J 7

SOUTH
- ♠ A J 9 8 7
- ♥ A K 3
- ♦ 9 7 2
- ♣ K 5

The bidding:

South	West	North	East
1 ♠	Pass	2 ♦	Pass
2 NT	Pass	3 NT	

Opening lead—six of clubs.

We have mentioned before that Sylvia was an accident-prone player. As a matter of fact, many of Sylvia's triumphs came about through some inadvertence on her part, whether because of an unintended carelessness, or by virtue of a gross misapprehension of what she conceived to be the governing principle of a hand.

These sensational triumphs, whatever their cause, were an unending topic of conversation among the members of the club. Everyone knew that Sylvia was a somewhat confused player who, due to the eccentricities of her thinking, might make the strangest bids or plays at any given moment. It wasn't that she didn't try to reason things out—according to her lights she was playing correctly—it was rather that her conclusions were incomprehensible by ordinary standards.

She was playing at the club one day when this hand came up. Sylvia was East. South got to three notrump and West led a club.

Sylvia took the ace and returned the jack. South, one of the club's top experts, won with the king. He saw that by far the best chance of making the hand was to rely on a spade finesse. If Sylvia had the king, he could finesse against her and bring home nine tricks.

South also saw that it would be foolish to try to capture five diamond tricks because that would require West to have both the king and jack. A single finesse (in spades) obviously had a better chance of succeeding than a double finesse (in diamonds).

So he led a diamond to the ace, preparing to take a spade finesse. But on the ace, Sylvia, who thought he intended to finesse the queen, played the king!

Unaware of Sylvia's mistake, South took stock again. Naturally, he thought the king was a singleton. So instead of finessing the spade, he returned to his hand with a heart and led the nine of diamonds and finessed against West's presumed jack.

Sylvia won the trick with the jack, returned a club, and South went down two!

Nothing
to
Lose

West dealer.
Both sides vulnerable.

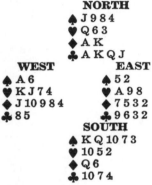

                    NORTH
                    ♠ J 9 8 4
                    ♥ Q 6 3
                    ♦ A K
                    ♣ A K Q J
WEST   **EAST**
♠ A 6   ♠ 5 2
♥ K J 7 4   ♥ A 9 8
♦ J 10 9 8 4   ♦ 7 5 3 2
♣ 8 5   ♣ 9 6 3 2
                    SOUTH
                    ♠ K Q 10 7 3
                    ♥ 10 5 2
                    ♦ Q 6
                    ♣ 10 7 4

The bidding:

West	North	East	South
Pass	1 ♣	Pass	1 ♠
Pass	3 ♠	Pass	4 ♠

Opening lead — jack of diamonds.

You don't see the declarer's cards when you are defending a contract, but that shouldn't stop you from making certain reasonable assumptions about the nature of his hand.

It is a basic principle of defense to assume that partner has the necessary cards or distribution that will permit the contract to be defeated. To play otherwise is a form of defeatism, and it cannot be right to play on the basis that you are licked before you start.

Here is a hand to illustrate the point. South was in four spades and West led a diamond. Declarer won it in dummy and led the jack of spades, losing to the ace. It was now up to West to make the only play that could defeat the contract.

He led the jack of hearts and then it did not matter what declarer did because he had to go down one. If South covered the jack with the queen, East would take the ace and return the nine to trap the ten and thus score three heart tricks, while if declarer ducked the jack lead, East would likewise duck and in this way score three heart tricks. So South went down one.

If West had led any heart but the jack, South would have made the contract. By playing properly, he could hold himself to two heart losers instead of three. And if West had not led a heart at all after taking the ace of spades, South would have made the hand easily.

West's heart lead was based on the assumption that East had to have the ace for the contract to be defeated. For West to credit South with the ace would have been equivalent to conceding the contract to him. The jack was selected as the heart to lead to cover the possibility that declarer had 10-x-x.

The jack play could conceivably have cost West a trick (if South had the ace), but it could not cost him the contract.

The
Seesaw
Play

South dealer.
North-South vulnerable.

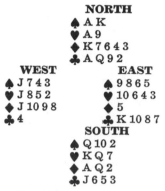

```
                    NORTH
                    ♠ A K
                    ♥ A 9
                    ♦ K 7 6 4 3
                    ♣ A Q 9 2
      WEST                        EAST
      ♠ J 7 4 3                   ♠ 9 8 6 5
      ♥ J 8 5 2                   ♥ 10 6 4 3
      ♦ J 10 9 8                  ♦ 5
      ♣ 4                         ♣ K 10 8 7
                    SOUTH
                    ♠ Q 10 2
                    ♥ K Q 7
                    ♦ A Q 2
                    ♣ J 6 5 3
```

The bidding:

South	West	North	East
1 ♣	Pass	2 ♦	Pass
2 NT	Pass	3 ♣	Pass
3 NT	Pass	6 NT	

Opening lead—jack of diamonds.

Declarer found an unusual way of making twelve tricks in this hand from a rubber bridge game, even though the cards were badly placed against him.

There didn't seem to be much to the play when dummy appeared. West led a diamond and South took it with the ace. Declarer continued with the queen of diamonds and would have had an easy time making the slam if the suit had been divided 3-2, but East showed out on the second diamond lead.

At this point, South might have taken a club finesse and relied on that suit to bring home three club tricks and the contract, but if he had done this, he would have been keenly disappointed. East's club holding would have been more than South could cope with, and he would have gone down one.

Instead, declarer chose a play that was bound to succeed regardless of how the clubs were divided. At trick three, he led a club to the ace, and then returned a low club from dummy.

East could not afford to go up with the king because that would have given South three tricks in each suit and the contract. So East played low on the club and declarer won with the jack, West showing out.

Declarer then shifted his attack back to diamonds, playing the king and another diamond, and thus made the slam, scoring three spades, three hearts, four diamonds and two clubs for twelve tricks.

The seesaw plays in diamonds and clubs were bound to succeed regardless of the club distribution. Suppose it had turned out that West was the one with the K-10-8-7 of clubs.

Then South's method of play would have been equally successful because, when East showed out on the second club lead, declarer would have had a marked finesse in clubs to pick up West's ten and would thus score three club tricks.

It just goes to show, as we've said before in this space, that the finesse is an instrument to be used sparingly.

Perfect Technique

South dealer.
Neither side vulnerable.

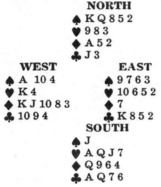

NORTH
♠ K Q 8 5 2
♥ 9 8 3
♦ A 5 2
♣ J 3

WEST
♠ A 10 4
♥ K 4
♦ K J 10 8 3
♣ 10 9 4

EAST
♠ 9 7 6 3
♥ 10 6 5 2
♦ 7
♣ K 8 5 2

SOUTH
♠ J
♥ A Q J 7
♦ Q 9 6 4
♣ A Q 7 6

The bidding:

South	West	North	East
1 ♥	2 ♦	2 ♠	Pass
2 NT	Pass	3 NT	

Opening lead—ten of clubs.

Here is a fine hand that illustrates the technique of good dummy play. It was played in the national Masters Individual many years ago.

West led the ten of clubs. Declarer covered with the jack and won the king with the ace. Then he played the jack of spades. If West had taken the ace, South's task would have been easier, but West properly ducked and the jack held the trick.

From South's viewpoint, nine tricks were still far, far away. He was short of entries to dummy and there weren't many tricks to develop even if he got there. At this point he led the jack of hearts, being careful to play the eight from dummy when West took the king.

West returned the nine of clubs, which South took with the queen. Declarer then cashed the ace of hearts, playing the nine from dummy, and exited with a club.

East took the seven with the eight and returned the seven of diamonds, covered by South with the nine. When West played the ten, South allowed him to hold the trick.

This effectively endplayed West. He could not play the ace and another spade, which would make dummy's spades good, nor could he lead the ten of spades first, because dummy would win and return a spade to accomplish the same result. So West returned the jack of diamonds.

Declarer won it with the queen, cashed the six of clubs, and led a diamond to the ace. He now played the three of hearts and finessed the seven when East followed low. The queen of hearts provided trick number nine.

Note that if the eight and nine of hearts had not been unblocked earlier, South would have gone down because he would have been unable to cash two hearts at the finish.

Note also that if East had returned a club at trick seven, instead of a diamond, South would have attained the same end position by leading the nine of diamonds.

A Necessary Switch

South dealer.
Neither side vulnerable.

```
                NORTH
                ♠ Q 5 4
                ♥ A J
                ♦ 9 6 4
                ♣ K Q J 9 2
   WEST                     EAST
♠ 10 7 6 2               ♠ A K J 8 3
♥ Q 10 9 7 3            ♥ K 6 2
♦ ———                   ♦ A 7 2
♣ 8 7 5 3              ♣ 6 4
                SOUTH
                ♠ 9
                ♥ 8 5 4
                ♦ K Q J 10 8 5 3
                ♣ A 10
```

The bidding:

South	West	North	East
1 ♦	Pass	2 ♣	2 ♠
3 ♦	3 ♠	5 ♦	

Opening lead—two of spades.

Why is it that some people play their cards well and others don't? Many factors determine one's skill in card play, but perhaps the most important of all is the ability to visualize the unseen hands.

To play well, seeing 52 cards, is no great feat; but to play well, seeing only 26 cards, is a knack developed by only a limited few.

Yet, it is not so difficult to play well if you go about it the right way. Take this hand, for instance, where East must have his thinking cap on to defeat the contract. Suppose he wins the spade lead with the jack and continues with the ace of spades, as most players would.

South would ruff the spade, force out the ace of diamonds, and then make the rest of the tricks, discarding his heart losers on dummy's clubs.

But if East is smart, he returns a heart at trick two and down goes the contract. Declarer winds up losing a spade, a heart and a diamond.

Now how is East supposed to figure out that the "dangerous" return of a heart is mandatory and that the "safe" return of a spade is really unsafe? Well, there are good reasons why East should shift to a heart.

He knows from the bidding that South has the ace of clubs. Without it South would not have an opening bid. He also knows that South has only one spade, because West indicated four-card spade length by opening his fourth-best spade.

A spade continuation is therefore futile because declarer will ruff it, lead trumps, and eventually score eleven tricks, discarding his losing hearts on dummy's clubs.

So East has to base his defense on the assumption that West has the queen of hearts. This is not a great deal to expect of West for his raise, and, in any case, no harm can come from the heart return even if South has the queen. Accordingly, East returns a heart at trick two, playing, in effect, as though he sees all 52 cards.

Rule of Eleven

North dealer.
Neither side vulnerable.

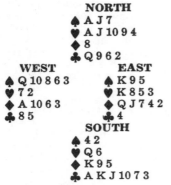

NORTH
♠ A J 7
♥ A J 10 9 4
♦ 8
♣ Q 9 6 2

WEST
♠ Q 10 8 6 3
♥ 7 2
♦ A 10 6 3
♣ 8 5

EAST
♠ K 9 5
♥ K 8 5 3
♦ Q J 7 4 2
♣ 4

SOUTH
♠ 4 2
♥ Q 6
♦ K 9 5
♣ A K J 10 7 3

The bidding:

North	East	South	West
1♥	Pass	2♣	Pass
3♣	Pass	5♣	

Opening lead—six of spades.

The Rule of Eleven is an extremely valuable gadget used primarily to assist the defense in the play of the cards. It depends for its application on the assumption that the card a defender leads is the fourth best card he has in that suit.

When the fourth best is led, whether on opening lead or during the later play, both the other defender and declarer can derive valuable knowledge by applying the Rule.

The application of the Rule is easy enough, since all it requires is elementary arithmetic. Perhaps the easiest way of demonstrating the Rule is by using the present hand as an example.

West leads his fourth best spade, the six. Declarer plays the seven from dummy in the hope of inducing East to make a mistake. If East is unfamiliar with the Rule, he may win the seven with the king, permitting declarer to make the contract later by finessing the jack and disposing of his heart loser on the ace.

To defeat the contract East must play his nine on the seven —and this is an easy enough play to make if he applies the Rule of Eleven. He subtracts the card led (the six) from eleven, and this tells him that the North, East and South hands together have five cards higher than the six.

Since East sees three of them in dummy and two of them in his own hand, he knows that South cannot have a spade higher than the six which was led.

The declarer can apply the Rule in a similar way. He knows that if the six is West's fourth best spade, East has precisely two spades higher than the six. This knowledge does not help declarer in the present hand, but there are many times when he can put the Rule to beneficial use.

Let's Look at the Facts

West dealer.
Neither side vulnerable.

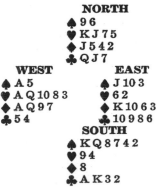

NORTH
♠ 9 6
♥ K J 7 5
♦ J 5 4 2
♣ Q J 7

WEST
♠ A 5
♥ A Q 10 8 3
♦ A Q 9 7
♣ 5 4

EAST
♠ J 10 3
♥ 6 2
♦ K 10 6 3
♣ 10 9 8 6

SOUTH
♠ K Q 8 7 4 2
♥ 9 4
♦ 8
♣ A K 3 2

The bidding:

West	North	East	South
1 ♥	Pass	Pass	2 ♠
Pass	2 NT	Pass	4 ♠

Opening lead—five of clubs.

The expert dummy player is sometimes compared to the fictional detective who makes it his business to ferret out every possible clue and then announces, near the end of the story, that the butler, or maybe the victim's great grandson, was the one who "done the old man in."

Of course, our heroic sleuth is always right — otherwise, there would be no story—and always presents with irrefutable logic the measured reasoning that led him to crack the case.

The declarer in this hand followed a similar format. He got to four spades on the optimistic sequence shown. While the two spade bid was probably all right, the jump to four was overdoing things a bit.

But having gotten there, our hero managed the affair quite well. He won the club lead with the jack and led the six of spades. When East followed with the three, he played the two. The six forced the ace, and that ended the hand for practical purposes. East-West later got a heart and a diamond, but South made four spades.

Of course, the normal way to handle the spade combination in this hand is for declarer to lead twice towards his K-Q in the hope that East was dealt either the A-x or A-x-x of spades.

But South reasoned that East could not have the ace of spades. The facts indicated otherwise. And once West was granted the ace of spades, it became pointless to waste the queen on the first spade play, since that play would surely lead to two trump losers. Instead, South had to hope that East had the J-10-x

The big clue was the opening lead. West could not sensibly have the A-K-Q of diamonds and lead a club originally. He would have led a diamond in such case. This meant that East had one of the diamond honors, most probably the king. It followed from this that East could not also have the ace of spades; if he had, he would not have passed West's opening bid.

Forcing a Count

South dealer.
Both sides vulnerable.

NORTH
♠ A J 10 4
♥ K 7 3
♦ K 6
♣ A J 10 9

WEST
♠ 3
♥ 8 6
♦ Q J 9 7 5 2
♣ K 7 6 2

EAST
♠ 8 5
♥ Q 9 5 4 2
♦ 8 3
♣ Q 8 4 3

SOUTH
♠ K Q 9 7 6 2
♥ A J 10
♦ A 10 4
♣ 5

The bidding:

South	West	North	East
1 ♠	Pass	3 ♣	Pass
3 ♠	Pass	4 ♠	Pass
4 NT	Pass	5 ♥	Pass
5 NT	Pass	6 ♥	Pass
7 ♠			

Opening lead—queen of diamonds.

Counting out a hand is a laborious process for most players, but it is not really difficult if you put your mind to it.

South is in seven spades and his only possible loser is a heart. The contract would not be difficult to make if he knew which opponent had the queen of hearts because all he would have to do in that case is finesse in the right direction.

But since he does not see where the queen is located, he should try to exhaust every avenue of approach before committing himself to the critical guess.

After winning the diamond lead with the ace and drawing two rounds of trumps, he cashes the ace of clubs and ruffs a club. A diamond to the king is followed by another club ruff, and then, after trumping a diamond in dummy, he ruffs the last club.

The purpose of these plays is to force the defenders to reveal their distribution. Thus, in the actual case, it becomes clear that West started with exactly one spade, six diamonds and four clubs. This information is gleaned as each defender follows or fails to follow suit.

South now knows that West must have been dealt exactly two hearts, neither more nor less. He likewise knows that East must therefore have been dealt precisely five hearts.

Declarer puts this knowledge to work by drawing the reasonable conclusion that East, who started with five hearts, is more likely to have been dealt the queen than West, who started with only two hearts. In fact, the odds, mathematically, are 5 to 2 that East's hand contains the queen of hearts.

Accordingly, South plays the jack of hearts to the king and then finesses the ten on the way back. As it happens, the finesse works and he makes the grand slam.

Of course, declarer cannot be sure that his method of play will succeed—heavy favorites sometimes lose—but he can do no better than follow the indicated odds.

A
Test
of Skill

North dealer.
Neither side vulnerable.

NORTH
- ♠ K 8 5
- ♥ Q 10
- ♦ K Q J 9 6 4
- ♣ K 10

WEST
- ♠ J 4 3 2
- ♥ 6 5 3
- ♦ 10 5
- ♣ 9 7 5 2

EAST
- ♠ Q 10 7 6
- ♥ A 4
- ♦ 8 7 2
- ♣ A Q J 3

SOUTH
- ♠ A 9
- ♥ K J 9 8 7 2
- ♦ A 3
- ♣ 8 6 4

The bidding:

North	East	South	West
1 ♦	Pass	1 ♥	Pass
2 ♦	Pass	3 ♥	Pass
4 ♥			

Opening lead—two of clubs.

It is not generally realized that a player ordinarily becomes declarer one deal out of four, dummy one deal out of four, and defender two deals out of four.

The role of the defense unfortunately does not receive as much attention as declarer's play, even though it is obvious that a player is a defender twice as often as he is a declarer. To defend well is just as important as to play the dummy well.

This hand comprises a good test of defensive skill. South is declarer at four hearts and West leads a club. East wins the king with the ace and the question is what he should play at trick two. Of course, he sees only his own hand and the dummy's.

The proper return is the four of hearts, and, in fact, this is the only card East can return to defeat the contract. Once East leads the low heart, declarer cannot make the hand regardless of how he plays; but if East leads any other card, South makes the contract.

Let's see why East's heart return is proper. He knows from the deuce of clubs lead that South has three clubs, all losers. West's deuce, presumably his fourth best club, marks declarer with the three missing clubs.

East also knows from the bidding that South must have the ace of spades and ace of diamonds for his jump to three hearts.

Putting this knowledge together, East can see it would be futile to lead the ace and another heart to prevent a club ruff in dummy, and that it would be equally futile to cash another club trick first.

Only by keeping trumps under control by underleading the ace of hearts can East hope to defeat the contract. East cannot be sure that this line of defense will stop the contract (which depends on South's distribution), but he must assume that the heart return offers the only chance of winning three clubs and a heart to beat the hand.

More About Percentages

East dealer.
Both sides vulnerable.

NORTH
♠ 10 4
♥ K Q J
♦ J 9 8 6 2
♣ Q 10 2

WEST
♠ Q 9 5 2
♥ 7
♦ K Q 10 5 4
♣ K 4 3

EAST
♠ K J 7 6
♥ 9 8 5 4 3
♦ 3
♣ J 7 6

SOUTH
♠ A 8 3
♥ A 10 6 2
♦ A 7
♣ A 9 8 5

The bidding:

East	South	West	North
Pass	1 NT	Pass	3 NT

Opening lead — king of diamonds.

This is the type of bothersome hand you run into from time to time when you are the declarer. You know very well you can make the contract regardless of how the East-West cards are divided, but the trouble is that you don't see the opponent's cards and therefore might misguage the situation and go down.

You win the diamond, of course, and the question is what to do next. There are seven tricks in sight and you need two more.

It is clear that it would be wrong to return a diamond. That would allow West to take the queen and make the obvious shift to spades. At the same time, the diamond return would establish only trick number eight.

By elimination, therefore, the suit to attack is clubs. Here there is a chance of gaining two tricks by playing the suit correctly. That's where the catch is—playing the suit correctly.

For example, you could play a low club towards dummy at trick two. If West followed low, you would then have to guess whether to play the ten or the queen. If West had the J-x-x, the ten play would be right, but if he had K-x-x the queen play would be right.

Such guesses have been known to turn hair prematurely gray, since it's pretty hard to guess right, under the circumstances, much more than 50% of the time. This type of guess should be avoided whenever possible, and, in the present hand, you should not subject yourself to such torture.

The proper play is to enter dummy with a heart and lead the ten (or queen) of clubs and finesse if East plays low. If West wins the king (as he would in the actual hand), nine tricks become assured. If West wins with the jack, the plan is to return to dummy and lead the queen and finesse again.

This method of play makes you at least a 3 to 1 favorite to fulfill the contract, and furthermore saves a lot of wear and tear on the nerves.

An Oddity

West dealer.
East-West vulnerable.

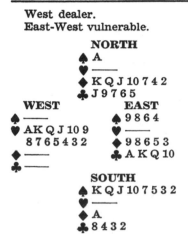

                    NORTH
                    ♠ A
                    ♥ —
                    ♦ K Q J 10 7 4 2
                    ♣ J 9 7 6 5
WEST   **EAST**
♠ —   ♠ 9 8 6 4
♥ A K Q J 10 9   ♥ —
♦ 8 7 6 5 4 3 2   ♦ 9 8 6 5 3
♣ —   ♣ A K Q 10
                    SOUTH
                    ♠ K Q J 10 7 5 3 2
                    ♥ —
                    ♦ A
                    ♣ 8 4 3 2

The bidding:

West	North	East	South
7 ♥	Pass	Pass	7 ♠

Opening lead—ace of hearts.

I once ran a hand in this column in which the distinguishing feature was that North, East, South and West each played an ace on the last trick! These plays, by the way, all made sense, and though the hand was not otherwise unusual, it was worthy of mention because of the peculiar ending.

A reader asks whether I am familiar with any hand where four aces are played on the first trick. Several hands of this type have been composed, and I offer here this curiosity published originally by the late and great Robert Darvas.

South is declarer at seven spades and West leads the ace of hearts. Observe what happens if South trumps in his hand instead of in dummy. East discards a diamond and South ruffs and cashes the ace of diamonds.

This does him no good, though, because when he enters dummy with a trump to discard all his clubs on the diamonds, he finds he can discard only three of them. On the next diamond, East ruffs, and South must then go down one.

Declarer's best play on the opening lead, therefore, is to ruff the ace of hearts with the ace of spades.

It does not matter what East plays on the trick, since he cannot stop the contract, so, to be sociable, he discards the ace of clubs.

South, of course, discards the ace of diamonds, and the opening trick thus consists of the ace of hearts from West, the ace of spades from North, the ace of clubs from East, and the ace of diamonds from South!

Declarer then cashes the K-Q-J-10 of diamonds, discarding four club losers, and thus fulfills his mission.

There is no moral connected with this tale, since the hand is purely imaginary and not likely to be dealt in real life, but if ever you are dealt one of these four hands, please play your part and play an ace on the opening trick!

Trump Echo

South dealer.
Both sides vulnerable.

```
                NORTH
              ♠ 10 8 4 3
              ♥ 8 7
              ♦ K Q J 8
              ♣ K Q 5
   WEST                    EAST
♠ 7 6 2                  ♠ A
♥ J 9 6 4 3             ♥ K Q 10 5 2
♦ 10 9 5 3             ♦ 7 4
♣ 9                     ♣ A 10 8 4 2
                SOUTH
              ♠ K Q J 9 5
              ♥ A
              ♦ A 6 2
              ♣ J 7 6 3
```

The bidding:

South	West	North	East
1 ♠	Pass	2 ♦	2 ♥
2 ♠	Pass	4 ♠	

Opening lead—nine of clubs.

Good defensive play rests heavily on partnership cooperation. The defenders work together as a team, helping each other in every conceivable way to solve the mystery of declarer's unseen hand. Only by guiding each other through the use of conventions and ordinary common sense can they hope to achieve a high degree of effectiveness.

Look at this hand, for example, where West leads a club. East doesn't have to be a genius to read the lead as a singleton. After all, he had bid hearts, and West presumably wouldn't lead a club instead of a heart unless he had a good reason. That reason, particularly in view of East's club length, has to be that the club is a singleton.

So East takes the ace and returns the ten of clubs. He chooses the ten, a high card, to show that he wants the high suit (as between hearts and diamonds) returned when West ruffs. This is a use of the suit-preference convention.

West trumps with the six of spades and obediently leads the four of hearts (his fourth-best heart). The queen loses to the ace and South leads the king of spades, West playing the two and East the ace.

At this point East has a critical decision to make. If he tries to cash the king of hearts, which he might be tempted to do, he hands South the contract. South would ruff and make the rest of the tricks.

But if he leads a club, West ruffs and South goes down.

How can East know which to lead? He would surely play a club if he knew West had another trump. But he knows that if declarer started with a six-card trump suit, West will not have a spade with which to ruff a club return.

Actually, East solves the problem quite easily. West earlier played the six and then the two of trumps. This high-low, called a trump echo, signals that he started with three trumps. East therefore returns a club to defeat the contract.

A Guaranteed Line of Play

East dealer.
North-South vulnerable.

```
                    NORTH
                  ♠ A 3
                  ♥ Q 8 3
                  ♦ K 8 5
                  ♣ K 8 7 6 2
      WEST                      EAST
    ♠ K 8 4                   ♠ Q J 10 9 7
    ♥ 7 4                     ♥ 5 2
    ♦ J 10 6 3 2              ♥ 6
    ♣ Q J 9                   ♦ A Q 9
                             ♣ 10 4
                    SOUTH
                  ♠ 6
                  ♥ A K J 10 9 5 2
                  ♦ 7 4
                  ♣ A 5 3
```

The bidding:

East	South	West	North
3 ♠	4 ♥	4 ♠	5 ♥

Opening lead—four of spades.

The most interesting hands to play are those where the issue is in doubt. The outcome may depend on luck, that is, the question of whether the opponents' cards are divided favorably or not; or it may depend on skill, that is, whether declarer can overcome an unlucky lie of the cards if it exists.

For example, take this hand. South is in five hearts and West leads a spade. Declarer takes the ace, draws two rounds of trumps, and then plays the A-K and another club.

Unfortunately, West wins the third club and shifts to the jack of diamonds. This spells disaster, because the defense wins two diamonds and a club to defeat the hand a trick.

South is unlucky in two respects. If East had had three clubs instead of West, he would have made the contract, since East could not successfully attack diamonds in that case. And if West had had the ace of diamonds instead of East, South would also have made the contract.

However, South can improve his chances considerably, and in the actual case make the hand, by adopting a slightly different line of play.

What he should do is play a low spade from dummy on the opening lead! This may look like an odd thing to do, but it cannot cost declarer anything to make the play and it gives him an extra chance to make the contract.

East wins the spade, but cannot defeat the contract regardless of what he returns. (As a matter of fact, if he does not cash the ace of diamonds at this point, he loses it.)

Suppose he returns a spade. Declarer discards a club, draws two rounds of trumps, cashes the A-K of clubs, and ruffs a club. This establishes two club tricks for him, and it is a simple matter to enter dummy with a trump and discard two diamonds on the 8-7 of clubs.

All that declarer has to do, really, is think of the right way to play at trick one.

Double Dummy Problem

West dealer.
Both sides vulnerable.

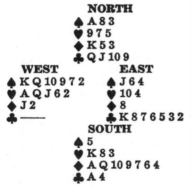

```
                    NORTH
                    ♠ A 8 3
                    ♥ 9 7 5
                    ♦ K 5 3
                    ♣ Q J 10 9
      WEST                     EAST
   ♠ K Q 10 9 7 2           ♠ J 6 4
   ♥ A Q J 6 2             ♥ 10 4
   ♦ J 2                   ♦ 8
   ♣ ——                    ♣ K 8 7 6 5 3 2
                    SOUTH
                    ♠ 5
                    ♥ K 8 3
                    ♦ A Q 10 9 7 6 4
                    ♣ A 4
```

The bidding:

West	North	East	South
1♠	Pass	2♣	2♦
2♥	3♦	Pass	5♦

Opening lead—king of spades.

This deal occurred in the 1964 World Olympiad match between the Philippines and the Republic of China. You may not approve of the bidding—East's two club response s e e m s exceptionally light — but that's the way it went.

West led the king of spades and the Chinese declarer (Chien Hwa Wang) had a difficult problem to solve. While it seemed likely that the club finesse would succeed, there was a grave danger of losing three heart tricks to go down one.

Wang solved the problem in a remarkable fashion. At trick one

he played the three of spades from dummy and the five from his hand!

As a result of this extraordinary play, the contract could not be defeated. West continued with the queen of spades and declarer followed low again from dummy, ruffing in his hand with the six.

Wang then cashed the ace of diamonds, entered dummy by playing the seven to the king, led the queen of clubs, and finessed when East followed low.

When the finesse succeeded, declarer continued his extraordinary line of play by leading the ace of spades from dummy and discarding his ace of clubs on it!

Wang then led the jack of clubs from dummy, trapping East's king, and, when East covered, South ruffed with the nine, returned to dummy by playing his four of diamonds to the five, and discarded two of his hearts on the 10-9 of clubs. The only tricks Wang lost were a spade and a heart.

If you don't think this was a virtuoso performance by Wang, try the hand on your bridge-playing friends, showing them all 52 cards, and challenge them to make five diamonds with the North-South cards. If they succeed, you might be better off if you stopped playing bridge with them!

The Alcatraz Coup

North dealer.
Both sides vulnerable.

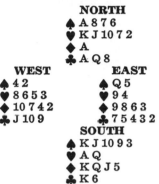

NORTH
♠ A 8 7 6
♥ K J 10 7 2
♦ A
♣ A Q 8

WEST
♠ 4 2
♥ 8 6 5 3
♦ 10 7 4 2
♣ J 10 9

EAST
♠ Q 5
♥ 9 4
♦ 9 8 6 3
♣ 7 5 4 3 2

SOUTH
♠ K J 10 9 3
♥ A Q
♦ K Q J 5
♣ K 6

The bidding:

North	East	South	West
1 ♥	Pass	2 ♠	Pass
4 ♠	Pass	4 NT	Pass
5 ♠	Pass	7 ♠	

Opening lead—jack of clubs.

The Ethics Committee at Alcatraz was in solemn session. The chairman, having introduced the disputants (South and East) to the committee, stated that the facts had been agreed upon in advance and that all that remained for the committee to rule on was the conduct and ethics of the prisoners.

South had become declarer that afternoon at seven spades and West had led a club. South realized at once that the outcome depended solely on finding the queen of trumps, and so, in a stroke of unprecedented brilliance, he announced, before playing from dummy, that he had 100 honors. At the same time he eyed his opponents furtively in order to study their reaction to this amazing statement.

However, East was not far behind declarer in gamesmanship. He immediately reached for his pencil and gravely entered 100 points in the North-South column of the scoresheet.

This was all the information that South needed on how to play the trumps. Accordingly, at trick two, he led the king of spades and followed this with the jack. When West played low, South confidently finessed, since East could not possibly have the queen of spades and still credit South with 100 honors.

But when East produced the queen; South (who was serving a term for having sold the Brooklyn Bridge to three different people) immediately let out a loud squawk and accused East of cheating. East's only response to this outburst was to transfer the 100-point entry from the North-South column to his own.

Apparently the standard of conduct practiced at Alcatraz is very different from what it is in the outside world, for the Ethics Committee not only praised both players highly for their ingenuity, but also awarded them each a place on the Alcatraz team in the forthcoming match against the San Quentin Grafters.

Quod
Erat
Demonstrandum

West dealer.
Both sides vulnerable.

```
                    NORTH
                  ♠ A K Q 3 2
                  ♥ 4 2
                  ♦ J 7
                  ♣ K Q 4 2
      WEST                      EAST
    ♠ 8                       ♠ 6 5
    ♥ A K J 10 8              ♥ 9 7 6 5 3
    ♦ K 10 9                  ♦ 8 5 4 2
    ♣ J 9 7 5                 ♣ A 8
                    SOUTH
                  ♠ J 10 9 7 4
                  ♥ Q
                  ♦ A Q 6 3
                  ♣ 10 6 3
```

The bidding:

West	North	East	South
1 ♥	Dble	2 ♥	2 ♠
3 ♥	3 ♠	Pass	4 ♠

Opening lead—king of hearts.

Here is an instructive hand. It shows there's much more to this game of bridge than generally meets the eye.

First, let's see how the hand was actually played. West led the king of hearts and continued with the ace. Declarer ruffed, drew two rounds of trumps, and then played a club towards dummy. East took the queen with the ace and returned a club to the king. Declarer then led the jack of diamonds and finessed, and West took it with the king and cashed his high club to defeat the contract a trick.

Of course, you could say that South was unlucky to find East with the ace of clubs over the K-Q, and West with the king of diamonds over the A-Q. However, while this is unquestionably true, the fact remains that declarer could have and should have made the hand despite the unlucky distribution.

Let's look at the bidding and see what South should have known about the adverse hands. Clearly, West needed more than just his heart suit to open the bidding with a heart. He was bound to have either the king of diamonds or ace of clubs for his opening bid.

Acting on this premise, South should have led a low diamond towards the jack after ruffing the heart and drawing two rounds of trumps.

If West had the king and played it, the contract would be made, since South would later be able to discard two clubs from dummy on the A-Q of diamonds. If West did not take the king, the only losers would be a heart and two clubs.

If West did not have the king, East would win the jack all right, but this, in turn, would mean that West had the ace of clubs. In that case, South would lose only one club trick (by leading clubs twice towards the K-Q), and make the contract with the loss of a heart, a diamond and a club.

A little thought, properly applied, can do a lot.

The Right Weapon at the Right Time

South dealer.
North-South vulnerable.

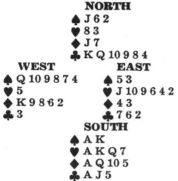

NORTH
♠ J 6 2
♥ 8 3
♦ J 7
♣ K Q 10 9 8 4

WEST
♠ Q 10 9 8 7 4
♥ 5
♦ K 9 8 6 2
♣ 3

EAST
♠ 5 3
♥ J 10 9 6 4 2
♦ 4 3
♣ 7 6 2

SOUTH
♠ A K
♥ A K Q 7
♦ A Q 10 5
♣ A J 5

The bidding:

South	West	North	East
2 ♥	2 ♠	3 ♣	Pass
4 NT	Pass	5 ♣	Pass
5 NT	Pass	6 ♦	Pass
7 NT			

Opening lead—three of clubs.

In bridge, as in war, all kinds of weapons are available to the contestants. The side with the superior weapons usually wins, but if the weapons are not deployed correctly, or the wrong ones are used, the theoretically inferior side may occasionally come out on top.

Examine this deal w h e r e South is in seven notrump. He appears to be outgunned—since he has only twelve sure tricks and the thirteenth seems to depend on a d i a m o n d finesse which is doomed to fail.

However, if South plays his cards right, he wins the battle.

He does not rely on that old standby, the finesse; he turns instead to a more sophisticated weapon—the squeeze.

On the bidding, he realizes that there is not much chance of the diamond finesse succeeding, and that there is an excellent chance of West's having both the queen of spades and king of diamonds.

Accordingly, South begins by cashing the A-K of spades, the A-K-Q of hearts, and six club tricks. When he leads the last club from dummy, this is the three-card position:

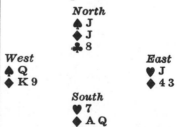

North
♠ J
♦ J
♣ 8

West
♠ Q
♦ K 9

East
♥ J
♦ 4 3

South
♥ 7
♦ A Q

East discards a diamond and South a heart. West cannot spare the queen of spades, so he also discards a diamond.

At this point South knows that East's last two cards are a heart and a diamond, and that West's last two cards are a spade and a diamond.

He consequently has no problem when he leads the diamond jack from dummy. He goes up with the ace, knowing the king will fall. It's like taking candy from a baby!

121

Even
If You Lose
You Win

South dealer.
North-South vulnerable.

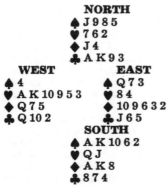

NORTH
♠ J 9 8 5
♥ 7 6 2
♦ J 4
♣ A K 9 3

WEST
♠ 4
♥ A K 10 9 5 3
♦ Q 7 5
♣ Q 10 2

EAST
♠ Q 7 3
♥ 8 4
♦ 10 9 6 3 2
♣ J 6 5

SOUTH
♠ A K 10 6 2
♥ Q J
♦ A K 8
♣ 8 7 4

The bidding:

South	West	North	East
1 ♠	2 ♥	2 ♠	Pass
3 ♠	Pass	4 ♠	

Opening lead—king of hearts.

One of declarer's most frequent problems is whether to finesse or play for the drop when he is missing four to the queen of a suit. There is ordinarily such a slight mathematical advantage in favor of playing for the drop that almost any clue which indicates otherwise should persuade declarer to finesse instead.

Here is an excellent example of declarer's proper approach to the play in a case where he can see that the fate of the hand depends on how he handles the trumps.

West cashes the K-A of hearts and continues with the ten, which South ruffs as East discards a diamond. Declarer cashes the ace of spades, both defenders following low, but since he is not yet ready for the crucial trump decision, he temporarily shifts his attention elsewhere to learn more about the opponents' distribution.

He leads a club to the king, a diamond to the king, a club to the ace, followed by a diamond to the ace. When he now ruffs a diamond in dummy and leads the jack of spades, East following low, declarer comes face to face with the decision of whether to finesse.

South still does not know where the queen is located, but, peculiarly enough, he can guarantee ten tricks by taking a finesse.

In the actual hand the finesse succeeds and South winds up making the contract, losing two hearts and a club, but the outcome would have been exactly the same had the finesse lost to the queen.

In that case, West — whose original distribution must have consisted of two spades, six hearts, three diamonds and two clubs—would be forced to return a heart, permitting South to discard his club loser as he ruffed the return in dummy.

In other words, South may lose the battle for the queen if he takes the finesse, but he is sure to win the war.

Stay Away
from the
Man With the Gun

South dealer.
North-South vulnerable.

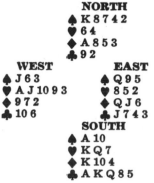

NORTH
♠ K 8 7 4 2
♥ 6 4
♦ A 8 5 3
♣ 9 2

WEST
♠ J 6 3
♥ A J 10 9 3
♦ 9 7 2
♣ 10 6

EAST
♠ Q 9 5
♥ 8 5 2
♦ Q J 6
♣ J 7 4 3

SOUTH
♠ A 10
♥ K Q 7
♦ K 10 4
♣ A K Q 8 5

The bidding:

South	West	North	East
2 NT	Pass	3 ♠	Pass
3 NT			

Opening lead—jack of hearts.

Most players show 22 to 24 high-card points with an opening two notrump bid, but even the most dogmatic of them would probably approve South's two notrump bid in this case, considering the clubs to be worth 1 or 2 points more than their face value.

However, they might not endorse South's method of play at three notrump. He won the jack of hearts with the king and cashed the A-K-Q of clubs. When West showed out, declarer, with fingers crossed, led another club, hoping to find the hearts favorably divided, but

East won the club and returned a heart to put the contract down one.

Of course, South would have made the hand had he found the clubs divided 3-3 or West with four of them, and to that extent he was unlucky.

However, his method of play was far from correct. Starting as he did with eight tricks, South should have taken better aim for his ninth trick.

His major concern should have been to try to avoid East's taking the lead for the potentially fatal heart return through the Q-7. All his efforts should have been addressed to this one possibility.

South should have entered dummy with a diamond at trick two and led a low club next. With East following low, South finesses the eight, not expecting the deep finesse to win, but attempting merely to establish his fifth club as the ninth trick.

As it happens, West wins the eight with the ten but cannot stop the contract whatever he returns. So South's thoughtful planning succeeds and he is rewarded for his care with nine tricks.

Note that this method of play succeeds whenever the clubs are divided 3-3, 4-2, or even when East has five or six to the J-10. It makes South a more than 10 to 1 favorite to make the contract.

123

The Odds
Are
2 to 1

South dealer.
North-South vulnerable.

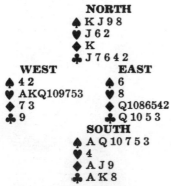

NORTH
♠ K J 9 8
♥ J 6 2
♦ K
♣ J 7 6 4 2

WEST
♠ 4 2
♥ A K Q 10 9 7 5 3
♦ 7 3
♣ 9

EAST
♠ 6
♥ 8
♦ Q 10 8 6 5 4 2
♣ Q 10 5 3

SOUTH
♠ A Q 10 7 5 3
♥ 4
♦ A J 9
♣ A K 8

The bidding:

South	West	North	East
1 ♠	4 ♥	4 ♠	Pass
6 ♠			

Opening lead—king of hearts.

Here is a fine hand where good play enabled declarer to bring home a slam.

West led the king of hearts and continued with the ace. Declarer ruffed, drew two rounds of trumps, cashed the king of diamonds, and ruffed dummy's last heart. Then, after cashing the ace of diamonds, he ruffed the jack in dummy.

South now had to save the potential club loser or lose the contract. Had he cashed the A-K of clubs in the hope of catching either opponent with a singleton or doubleton queen, he would have gone down one.

But South realized there was a better chance of making the hand on a different method of play, and, backing his judgment, he led the jack of clubs, planning to finesse if East followed low. When East covered with the queen, South won with the king as West followed with the nine.

Declarer then returned to dummy with a trump, led a club and finessed the eight to make the slam.

South's highly unusual handling of the club suit was clearly correct because at the point when he led the jack of clubs he knew 12 of West's original 13 cards.

West had revealed an eight-card suit at trick two and had also followed twice in spades and diamonds, thus accounting in full for his holding in three suits. It consequently became certain that he held precisely one club.

This club could be either the queen, ten, nine, five or three. Since South knew he had no chance if it was the five or three, he had to assume it was the queen, ten or nine.

By leading the jack instead of a low club, declarer gave himself twice as much chance of making the contract, since West would normally be dealt the singleton ten or nine exactly twice as often as the singleton queen. In the actual case, the percentage play worked to perfection.

Insuring Your Chances

North dealer.
Neither side vulnerable.

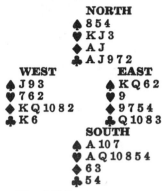

```
                NORTH
               ♠ 8 5 4
               ♥ K J 3
               ♦ A J
               ♣ A J 9 7 2
   WEST                    EAST
♠ J 9 3                  ♠ K Q 6 2
♥ 7 6 2                  ♥ 9
♦ K Q 10 8 2            ♦ 9 7 5 4
♣ K 6                    ♣ Q 10 8 3
                SOUTH
               ♠ A 10 7
               ♥ A Q 10 8 5 4
               ♦ 6 3
               ♣ 5 4
```

The bidding:

North	East	South	West
1♣	Pass	1♥	Pass
2♥	Pass	4♥	

Opening lead—king of diamonds.

Suit establishment is the process of manufacturing tricks that do not exist at the start of a hand. It is one of the most basic and essential skills in bridge, for, while the majority of tricks are won with aces, kings and queens, there is seldom a hand where at least some tricks are not won with low cards that have become established as winners.

South starts with nine winners—six hearts and three side aces. Clearly there is little hope for the contract unless dummy's long clubs can be developed so as to provide at least one additional trick.

However, before wading into the clubs, declarer should take note of a problem that often rears its head when suit establishment is under contemplation. He should make sure that he can cash the long club (or clubs) after establishing the suit.

Thus, if he wins the ace of diamonds and plays the ace and another club, he will fail in his purpose. West wins, cashes the diamond queen, and shifts to a spade. Declarer takes the ace, enters dummy with a trump and ruffs a club.

When the suit fails to divide 3-3, South is finished. He can cross to dummy with a heart and trump the fourth round of clubs, but he can no longer reach dummy to cash the fifth club.

Declarer can avoid this unsatisfying outcome by making use of a simple dodge. He should play a *low* club from dummy at trick two instead of the ace.

The defense takes the club, cashes a diamond, and shifts to a spade. South wins, plays the ace and another club, ruffing high, cashes the A-K of hearts, and ruffs dummy's fourth club high. The jack of hearts provides the entry to cash the fifth club.

The suggested method of play succeeds whether the clubs are divided 3-3 or 4-2, and more than doubles the chance of making the contract.

Still More About Queens

North dealer.
East-West vulnerable.

NORTH
♠ 10 5
♥ A 9 4
♦ K Q 6
♣ A J 10 5 4

WEST
♠ A Q 8 7
♥ 3
♦ J 7 5 3 2
♣ Q 8 2

EAST
♠ K J 9 6 4 2
♥ Q 10 6
♦ A 9 4
♣ 7

SOUTH
♠ 3
♥ K J 8 7 5 2
♦ 10 8
♣ K 9 6 3

The bidding:

North	East	South	West
1♣	1♠	2♥	3♠
4♥	4♠	5♥	

Opening lead—ace of spades.

Let's say you're declarer at five hearts and West leads the ace and another spade, which you ruff.

The situation is not entirely promising. You are bound to lose a diamond, come what may, so to make the contract you will have to play both the hearts and the clubs without loss, even though you are missing four to the queen of each suit.

Ordinarily, you would play for the drop, which is the mathematically recommended method when missing four to the queen. You would hope the A-K will catch the queen on the first or second round.

But playing for the drop would not be a smart move in the present case. The opponents did voluntarily bid four spades, and it is reasonable to suppose that they would not have done so if they each had two hearts and two clubs to lose on top of two diamonds—for in that case they would be subjecting themselves to an 800-point penalty.

It follows from this that either one or the other of the opponents will have singletons (possibly a void) in the key suits.

Accordingly, you lead a heart to the ace and return a heart on which East plays the ten. Consistent with your theory, you finesse the jack. West shows out, discarding a diamond, and you are greatly pleased to have surmounted the first hurdle.

The next problem is to deal with the clubs. Since you have already successfully played West for a singleton heart, you should forestall any possible charge of discrimination and assume that East is the defender who is short in clubs.

After drawing East's last trump, you cash the king of clubs and finesse the ten. This operation likewise proves to be a huge success, and the reward for having twice transgressed the mathematical percentages is that you make five hearts.

The Pollyanna Psychosis

South dealer.
East-West vulnerable.

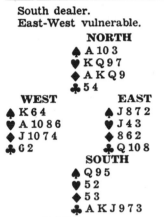

```
                     NORTH
                   ♠ A 10 3
                   ♥ K Q 9 7
                   ♦ A K Q 9
                   ♣ 5 4
    WEST                          EAST
  ♠ K 6 4                       ♠ J 8 7 2
  ♥ A 10 8 6                    ♥ J 4 3
  ♦ J 10 7 4                    ♦ 8 6 2
  ♣ 6 2                         ♣ Q 10 8
                     SOUTH
                   ♠ Q 9 5
                   ♥ 5 2
                   ♦ 5 3
                   ♣ A K J 9 7 3
```

The bidding:

South	West	North	East
1 ♣	Pass	1 ♦	Pass
2 ♣	Pass	2 ♥	Pass
3 ♣	Pass	3 ♠	Pass
3 NT	Pass	4 ♣	Pass
5 ♣	Pass	6 ♣	

Opening lead—four of diamonds.

I think we all occasionally look at a hand and overestimate its values.

Of course, steady overbidding is a serious fault for anybody to have. The same can also be said of any player who underbids regularly. The best policy is to bid hands for what they're worth, neither underbidding nor overbidding them, but this is hard to do consistently.

This hand was played in the match between Italy and the United States in 1951. Howard Schenken was playing South for the American team and opened the bidding with a club. True, it wasn't a high-class bid, but he decided to open the bidding, which was, of course, his right.

He found North with a big hand, and North never did let go until a slam was reached. Schenken did everything he could to slow down the proceedings, signing off repeatedly, but North had the bit firmly in his teeth, prizing his hand highly, and refused to heed the danger signals that Schenken kept hoisting.

The American team was very lucky on the deal because, with the East-West cards being distributed as they were, the slam could not be stopped.

West led a diamond. Schenken won it with the queen, finessed the jack of clubs, played a heart to the queen, and then drew two more rounds of trumps. When he led another heart, West took the ace, but that was the end of the hand because Schenken by now had twelve sure tricks.

Schenken would probably have been defeated if West had had the queen of clubs, or if the clubs had been divided 4-1, or if East had had the ace of hearts, or if East had had the king of spades and West had led a spade originally.

North was very pleased by the fortunate outcome of the hand, which was directly traceable to his optimistic series of bids.

I know. . . . I was North.

INDEX